Reading/Writing Companion

Mc
Graw
Hill

mheducation.com/prek-12

Send all inquiries to:
McGraw Hill
1325 Avenue of the Americas
New York, NY 10019

ISBN: 978-1-26-577227-7
MHID: 1-26-577227-4

Printed in the United States of America.

3 4 5 6 7 8 9 LMN 26 25 24 23 22   A

Welcome to WONDERS!

We're here to help you set goals to build on the amazing things you already know. We'll also help you reflect on everything you'll learn.

Let's start by taking a look at the incredible things you'll do this year.

You'll build knowledge on exciting topics and find answers to interesting questions.

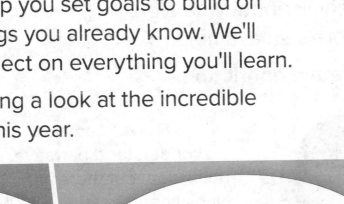

You'll read fascinating fiction, informational texts, and poetry and respond to what you read with your own thoughts and ideas.

And you'll research and write stories, poems, and essays of your own!

Here's a sneak peek at how you'll do it all.

"Let's go!"

You'll explore new ideas by reading groups of different texts about the same topic. These groups of texts are called *text sets*.

At the beginning of a text set, we'll help you set goals on the My Goals page. You'll see a bar with four boxes beneath each goal. Think about what you already know to fill in the bar. Here's an example.

I can read and understand narrative nonfiction.

I haven't read narrative nonfiction before. I'll shade in the **first box**.

I think I can do this, but I want more practice. I'll shade in the first **two boxes**.

I have read and understood narrative nonfiction, but there are more things I need to know. I'll shade in the first **three boxes**.

I can teach a friend all about narrative nonfiction. I'll shade in all **four boxes**.

As you move through a text set, you'll explore an essential question and build your knowledge of a topic until you're ready to write about it yourself.

You'll also learn skills that will help you reach your text set goals. At the end of lessons, you'll see a new Check In bar with four boxes.

CHECK IN 1 2 3 4

Reflect on how well you understood a lesson to fill in the bar.

Here are some questions you can ask yourself.

- Was I able to complete the task?

- Was it easy, or was it hard?

- Do I think I need more practice?

You have plenty of tools and resources to learn more, such as anchor charts and center activities. You can also reread a lesson or ask a teacher or peer for help.

It's okay if I think I need more practice. The most important thing is that I do my best and keep learning!

Thinking about what works best for me will help me choose what to do next.

At the end of each text set, you'll show off the knowledge you built by completing a fun task. Then you'll return to the second My Goals page where we'll help you reflect on all that you learned.

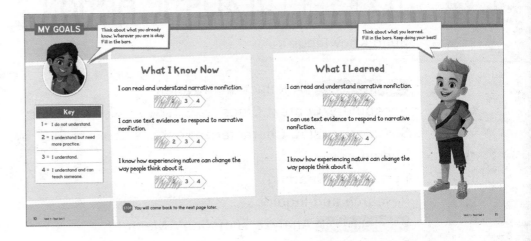

I'll fill in a new set of bars to show how far I've come. I started at 2, but now I'm at 4 because I can read and understand narrative nonfiction well enough to teach a friend.

I'll follow the same steps as I write my own stories, essays, and poems. I own my learning, and you can own yours!

"Let's get started!"

TEXT SET 1 **REALISTIC FICTION**

TEXT SET 2 **EXPOSITORY TEXT**

TEXT SET 3 **ARGUMENTATIVE TEXT**

EXTENDED WRITING

CONNECT AND REFLECT

 Digital Tools

Find this eBook and
other resources at
my.mheducation.com

Nigel Smith/SuperStock/Getty Images

TEXT SET 1 **BIOGRAPHY**

TEXT SET 2 **DRAMA**

TEXT SET 3 **POETRY**

EXTENDED WRITING

CONNECT AND REFLECT

 Digital Tools

Find this eBook and other resources at **my.mheducation.com**

Build Knowledge

? **Essential Question**

What can learning about different cultures teach us?

Build Vocabulary

Write new words you learned about what learning a new culture can teach us. Draw lines and circles for the words you write.

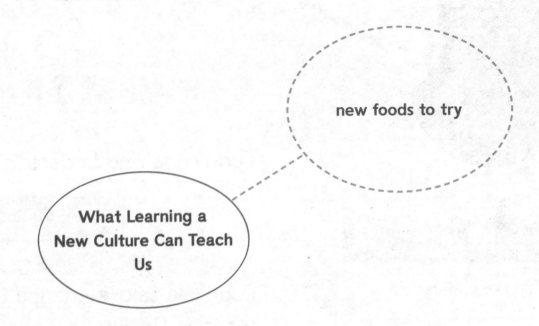

new foods to try

What Learning a New Culture Can Teach Us

Go online to **my.mheducation.com** and read the "A Special Day" Blast. Think about celebrations from other countries. What can we learn from these celebrations? Then blast back your response.

Think about what you already know. Fill in the bars. This will be a good start.

What I Know Now

Key

1 =	I do not understand.
2 =	I understand but need more practice.
3 =	I understand.
4 =	I understand and can teach someone.

I can read and understand realistic fiction.

I can use text evidence to respond to realistic fiction.

I know what learning about different cultures can teach us.

 You will come back to the next page later.

Think about what you learned.
Fill in the bars. What are you getting better at?

What I Learned

I can read and understand realistic fiction.

I can use text evidence to respond to realistic fiction.

I know what learning about different cultures can teach us.

My Goal I can read and understand realistic fiction.

TAKE NOTES

As you read, make note of interesting words and important events.

A Reluctant **TRAVELER**

PASSPORT

United States of America

Essential Question

?

What can learning about different cultures teach us?

Read about what Paul discovers in Argentina and what he learns about himself.

(bkgd) Alan SCHEIN/Alamy; (l) Clement Mok/Photodisc/Getty Images; (r) Tom Chance/Westend61/Getty Images

"I think packing winter clothes in August is weird," Paul said, looking from his bedroom window onto West 90th Street. This wasn't going to be a fun vacation. He was sure of it.

His mom **contradicted**, "It's not weird, honey. Argentina's in the Southern Hemisphere, and we're in the Northern Hemisphere, so the seasons are opposite." To Paul, this was just another reason to want to stay in New York City. Paul wanted to spend the rest of his summer break hanging out with his friends, and not with Aunt Lila and Uncle Art in a faraway country.

Paul's parents, Mr. and Mrs. Gorski, were teachers, and this was a chance they couldn't pass up. Their apartment had been covered with travel guides full of **cultural** information ever since Mrs. Gorski's sister and her husband had relocated to Argentina six months ago. The Gorskis had big plans. Paul, on the other hand, wanted to sleep late and play soccer with his friends. They lived in a city already. Why were they going to Buenos Aires?

As their plane took off, Paul's dad said, "Look down there! That's the island of Manhattan. See? You can even see Central Park!" Paul never realized how surrounded by water New York was. Many hours later, as the plane was landing in Buenos Aires, Paul noticed similar outlines of a city on the water, and bright lights, just like home.

Cartesia/Photodisc/Getty Images

FIND TEXT EVIDENCE 🔍

Read

Paragraphs 1–2

Plot: Characterization

What can you infer about how Paul feels from what he says?

He doesn't feel excited for going to Argentina because he said its weird.

Draw a box around the text that confirms how Paul feels.

Paragraphs 3–4

Theme

How does Paul feel and how do his parents feel about the trip?

Paul isn't into going to Argentina but his parents are.

Reread

Author's Craft

What does Paul's reaction to going to Argentina suggest?

"We have so much to show you!" Aunt Lila gushed when they met at the airport. They had a late dinner at a restaurant, just as they often did back home. But the smells coming from its kitchen were new. Uncle Art ordered in Spanish for everyone: *empanadas* (small meat pies), followed by *parrillada* (grilled meat), *chimichurri* (spicy sauce), and *ensalada mixta* (lettuce, tomatoes, and onions).

Paul made a face. "Don't be **critical,** Paul," his mom said. "Just take a taste." Though some of the foods were new, the spices and flavors were familiar to Paul.

"Mom, I had something like this at César's house," Paul said, after biting into an empanada. "This is really good." As he was **complimenting** the food, Paul felt his bleak mood improving.

Their first full day in Buenos Aires brought a rush of new sights, sounds, and languages. Paul noticed that like New York, Buenos Aires had people from all over the world. His Aunt Lila remarked, "We speak Spanish, but I really need to be multilingual!"

On a plaza, Paul saw a group of people dancing to music he'd never heard. Paul had seen breakdancing on the street, but never dancing like this. "That's the tango," Uncle Art said. "It's the dance Argentina is famous for! Being a soccer player, Paul, I know you have an **appreciation** for people who move well."

"You know, that is pretty cool," Paul admitted.

Around noon, they piled back into the car and drove to the most unusual neighborhood Paul had seen yet. All the buildings were painted or decorated in yellow and blue. "Soccer season has started here," his Aunt Lila said.

"Huh?" Paul asked, wondering if there had been a **misunderstanding.** "Isn't it too cold for soccer?" he asked.

"It's nearly spring. And," his aunt added, "Boca and River are playing at La Bombonera, the famous stadium, this afternoon." She held out her hand, which held five tickets to see these big teams play. Paul couldn't believe it.

"We're in the neighborhood of La Bombonera," Uncle Art said. "When Boca beats their rival, River, the people decorate their neighborhood in Boca colors!"

"Maybe I could paint my room in soccer team colors!" Paul **blurted.**

His mom smiled. "I **congratulate** you, Paul! You've turned out to be a really great traveler." Paul smiled, too.

Summarize

Use your notes to summarize important details of Paul's trip to Buenos Aires.

(b) Marcos Brindicci/reuters/Alamy Stock Photo; (t) Peter Horree/Alamy Stock Photo

---

FIND TEXT EVIDENCE 🔍

Read

Paragraphs 1-4

Summarize

Summarize Paul's reaction to what he saw and heard on the drive.

_____

_____

_____

_____

Paragraphs 5-7

Theme

How does Paul's perspective change by the end of the story? **Underline** text evidence.

At first, Paul didn't want to go to

_____

Reread

Author's Craft

Do you think "The Reluctant Traveler" is a good title for this story? Explain your answer.

Vocabulary

Use the example sentences to talk with a partner about each word. Then answer the questions.

appreciation

Gram showed her **appreciation** for my help by giving me a hug.

How do you show appreciation for someone's help?

I say "thank you" and give
them something in return.

blurted

By mistake, I **blurted** out the secret about the surprise.

How do you feel if you have blurted out a secret?

I feel embarrassed and stupid.

complimenting

Complimenting me when I do well makes me feel great.

If you were complimenting a friend, what would you say?

I would say "great job"
and "keep it up"

congratulate

After Niki lost the game, she went over to **congratulate** the winner.

What might you congratulate someone for?

For winning the
science Olympiad
competition.

contradicted

The children **contradicted** each other when they explained how the lamp broke.

Why might people have contradicted themselves?

Build Your Word List Pick a word you found interesting in the selection you read. Look up synonyms and antonyms of the word in a thesaurus and write them in your reader's notebook.

critical

A **critical** person often finds fault with what others do and points it out.

When have you been critical of yourself?

_____

_____

_____

cultural

Languages, foods, and celebrations are examples of **cultural** differences.

Give two examples of cultural activities.

_____

_____

_____

misunderstanding

Mira arrived at the show an hour late as a result of a **misunderstanding**.

How would you handle a misunderstanding with a friend?

_____

_____

Context Clues

When you don't know the meaning of an unfamiliar or multiple-meaning word, you can look for **cause-and-effect relationships** between words as clues to determine the word's meaning. Cause-and-effect clues may be within or beyond the same sentence as the unknown word.

FIND TEXT EVIDENCE

To understand what hemisphere *means, I can look at a cause-and-effect relationship.* Hemisphere *has to do with a location on Earth. Since seasons in the Northern and Southern hemispheres are opposite,* hemisphere *must refer to areas divided by the equator.*

"Argentina's in the Southern hemisphere, and we're in the Northern hemisphere, so the seasons are opposite."

Your Turn Use cause-and-effect relationships as clues to the meanings of the following words from "A Reluctant Traveler."

relocated, page 13 _to move from l place to another_

bleak, page 14 _____

CHECK IN 1 2 3 4

Summarize

When you summarize a story, you restate, or tell in your own words, the most important plot events and details in order. This helps you remember what you have read. It will also help to develop and deepen your understanding of the story. You can summarize a story after you've finished it, or summarize parts of a story while you are reading it.

 FIND TEXT EVIDENCE

Monitor your understanding of the opening of "A Reluctant Traveler" on page 13 by summarizing the most important plot events and details.

Page 13

"I think packing winter clothes in August is weird," Paul said, looking from his bedroom window onto West 90th Street. This wasn't going to be a fun vacation. He was sure of it.

His mom **contradicted**, "It's not weird, honey. Argentina's in the Southern hemisphere, and we're in the Northern hemisphere, so the seasons are opposite." To Paul, this was just another reason to want to stay in New York City.

> **Quick Tip**
>
> Summarizing helps you to monitor, or check, comprehension. If you have trouble summarizing, reread the story. Asking yourself questions about the text can also help you to summarize important details.

As the story begins, Paul is packing to go on a family vacation in Argentina. He doesn't understand why he needs winter clothes in August. His mom explains why the seasons are different between New York and Argentina.

 Your Turn Summarize Paul's first night in Buenos Aires and how the experiences affect him.

At first, Paul was bleak about Buenos Aires, but after experiencing the food and seeing the tango dance, he started to enjoy the trip more.

CHECK IN 1 > 2 > 3 > 4

Plot: Characterization

"A Reluctant Traveler" is realistic fiction. Realistic fiction tells about characters that are like real people and includes their relationships and conflicts. The story happens in a setting that is real or seems real and has events that could happen in real life. Authors of realistic fiction often include dialogue to develop characters' personalities. Dialogue also reveals characters' perspectives, or attitudes, about ideas.

FIND TEXT EVIDENCE

"A Reluctant Traveler" is realistic fiction. Paul and his parents travel from New York City to Buenos Aires, which are real places. Visiting relatives could happen in real life. The dialogue shows what real people might say.

Readers to Writers

Dialogue often reveals the thoughts and feelings of a character. It can also help readers analyze conflicts among characters. For example, Paul makes a face after his uncle orders the local food. Paul's mother says, "Don't be critical," and tells him to take a taste. This conflict shows that Paul and his mother start out with different ideas about visiting new places. Think about how you can use dialogue in your own writing.

Page 13

" I think packing winter clothes in August is weird," Paul said, looking from his bedroom window onto West 90th Street. This wasn't going to be a fun vacation. He was sure of it.

His mom **contradicted**, "It's not weird, honey. Argentina's in the Southern Hemisphere, and we're in the Northern Hemisphere, so the seasons are opposite." To Paul, this was just another reason to want to stay in New York City. Paul wanted to spend the rest of his summer break hanging out with his friends, and not with Aunt Lila and Uncle Art in a faraway country.

Paul's parents, Mr. and Mrs. Gorski, were teachers, and this was a chance they couldn't pass up. Their apartment had been covered with travel guides full of **cultural** information ever since Mrs. Gorski's sister and her husband had relocated to Argentina six months ago. The Gorskis had big plans. Paul, on the other hand, wanted to sleep late and play soccer with his friends. They lived in a city already. Why were they going to Buenos Aires?

As their plane took off, Paul's dad said, "Look down there! That's the island of Manhattan. See? You can even see Central Park!" Paul never realized how surrounded by water New York was. Many hours later, as the plane was landing in Buenos Aires, Paul noticed similar outlines of a city on the water, and bright lights, just like home.

Dialogue

Dialogue is the exact words the characters say.

Dialogue is shown using quotation marks.

A new paragraph indicates a different speaker.

Your Turn Read aloud a line of dialogue in "A Reluctant Traveler." How is the dialogue realistic? What does the line reveal about the character?

The dialogue thoughts in the first line shows Paul doesn't want

CHECK IN 1 2 3 4

Theme

The **theme** of a story is a big idea or message about life that the author wants to share. A story may have one theme or multiple themes. Themes may be implied, or not stated directly. To find the implied theme, note what characters think, say, and do. Also, the characters' perspectives often help to develop the theme.

 FIND TEXT EVIDENCE

In the first paragraph on page 13 of "A Reluctant Traveler," I see that Paul is not looking forward to his summer vacation. In the next paragraph, I see that his parents are taking him to Argentina to visit his aunt and uncle.

Quick Tip

Since themes may not be directly stated, you must make inferences. Ask yourself, "How does the setting advance the plot? What conflicts do the characters face and how do they respond? What do the characters learn? What message is the author giving readers?" Knowing these details helps to develop a theme.

What Does the Character Think, Say, or Do?	What Is the Character's Perspective?
Paul looks through his window. He says, ""I think packing winter clothes in August is weird."	Paul doesn't want to leave New York City. He'd rather sleep late and see his friends.

Theme

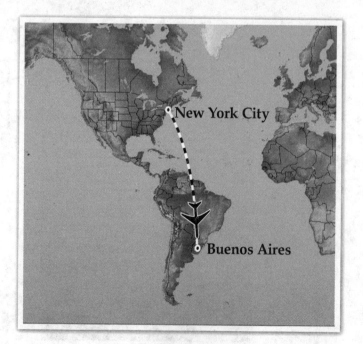

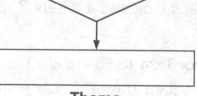 **Your Turn** Reread "A Reluctant Traveler." Complete the graphic organizer on page 21 by recording the most important things the characters think, say, or do and their perspectives. Include specific ideas in the text. Then state a theme of the story in the last box.

CHECK IN 1 2 3 4

What Does the Character Think, Say, or Do?

What Is the Character's Perspective?

Paul tastes the food in Beunos Aires and likes it.

Paul also the fest sees the tango dance and admits its cool and

Theme

When you try new things, you can get

an open mind, cause you never know if you'll like it or not.

Respond to Reading

Discuss the prompt below. Use your notes and text evidence to support your ideas.

What does the author want readers to understand about Paul by describing his experience from beginning to end?

_____

_____

_____

_____

_____

_____

_____

_____

_____

_____

_____

_____

Quick Tip

Use these sentence starters to retell the story and to organize ideas.

- *In the beginning of the story. . .*
- *The author shows Paul changing by. . .*
- *At the end, the author. . .*

Grammar Connections

As you write your response, make sure that the subjects of your sentences agree with your verbs.

Singular

*The **smell** from the kitchen **is** familiar.*

Plural

*The **smells** from the kitchen **are** familiar.*

CHECK IN 1 2 3 4

Learning About Different Cultures

COLLABORATE

In many countries, people of different cultures have their own customs and traditions and celebrate events differently. Choose one group of people to research its celebrations, customs, and traditions. Then create a pamphlet that presents and summarizes the information. Work collaboratively with a partner.

Step 1 **Set a Goal** Think about the purpose of your research. Which celebrations, customs, and traditions do you want to focus on?

_____

Step 2 **Identify Sources** Discuss how you will gather information from print sources, websites, or people. For a formal inquiry, use valid sources. For an informal inquiry, ask and clarify questions.

What else would help you identify and gather information from a variety of sources?

_____

Step 3 **Find and Record Information** Take notes on the information you gathered. Cite your sources so you can refer to them later.

Step 4 **Organize and Synthesize Information** Make an outline. See the partial outline above if you need help. Plan what to include in your pamphlet, such as photographs and captions. These text features can help emphasize or clarify information.

Step 5 **Create and Present** Use your outline to create your pamphlet. After you finish, present your work to the class.

A. Celebrations
1. food
2. music
3. dance

The partial outline above shows one student's categories to help focus her research about celebrations.

Quick Tip

A formal inquiry means using primary and secondary sources, such as encyclopedias, books, magazines, and websites for historical and present-day information. An informal inquiry means talking to people, such as neighbors or relatives, to get information. The adults you talk to during informal inquiry can help you develop and follow a research plan.

CHECK IN 〉 1 〉 2 〉 3 〉 4

They Don't Mean It!

Literature Anthology:
pages 182–193

? How does the author show that Mary's mother does not feel like she is being true to her culture?

Talk About It Reread paragraph 5 on **Literature Anthology** page 184. Turn to a partner and talk about how Mary describes her mother.

Cite Text Evidence What clues show that Mary's mother is not keeping her Chinese traditions? Write text evidence in the chart.

 Evaluate Information

The author uses the expression "made her soft" to describe Mary's mother. Think about what it means to become "soft." Why would readers think that Mrs. Yang is not becoming soft?

Clue	Clue	Clue

Why It's Important

Write I know that Mary's mother feels like she is not being true to her culture because the author _____

_____

_____

How does the author use dialogue to help you understand Mary's perspective about American customs?

 Talk About It Reread paragraphs 4-6 on **Literature Anthology** page 187. Turn to a partner and talk about what Mary and her mother discuss.

Cite Text Evidence What do Mary and her mother say and how does it show how she feels? Write text evidence in the chart.

Text Evidence	What It Shows

Write The author uses dialogue to help me infer that Mary feels

_____

_____

_____

_____

Quick Tip

Use these sentence starters to help you talk about the conflict between Mary and her mother.

- *The dialogue shows that Mary is worried about . . .*
- *I read that dessert is . . .*

 Make Inferences

Paying attention to the characters' relationships with one another will help you infer information about them. In paragraph 4, think about why Mary doesn't tell Mrs. O'Meara how much work it was to make the salad. What does this tell you about the kind of person Mary is?

? How does the author use the illustration to show how Mrs. Yang has changed?

Talk About It Reread paragraph 4 on **Literature Anthology** page 193. Use clues from the text and illustration to discuss what Mrs. Yang does.

Cite Text Evidence What clues in the text and illustration help you see how Mrs. Yang has changed? Write evidence in the chart.

Quick Tip

When you read a text, analyze the author's use of text features, such as illustrations. Paying close attention to how the characters are shown will help you understand how they feel.

Text Evidence	Illustration Clues	What It Shows

Write The author uses the illustration to show that Mrs. Yang has

changed by _____

_____

_____

_____

_____

CHECK IN 1 2 3 4

Respond to Reading

COLLABORATE

Discuss the prompt below. Use your notes and text evidence to support your response.

What message does the author want to send by sharing the experiences of different cultures?

_____

_____

_____

_____

_____

_____

_____

_____

_____

_____

Sergej Razvodovskij/Shutterstock.com

Quick Tip

Use these sentence starters to help organize your text evidence.

- *When the Yangs first moved to America, they felt . . .*

- *It is important for the families to interact because . . .*

- *Kim's and Mary's families learned that . . .*

CHECK IN 1 2 3 4

Where Did That Come From?

Literature Anthology:
pages 196–197

From Bite...

1.   Food is one of the most common ways people have shared cultures. Dishes we think of as American have in fact come from all over the world. Hamburgers were crafted by German immigrants. Macaroni was rolled out by Italians. Apple pie was first served not in America but England.

...To Beat

2.   People from different backgrounds have also drummed distinct sounds into the music we hear today. Hip hop and rap, for example, have been traced to West African and Caribbean storytelling. Salsa music comes from a type of Cuban music called "son," which has been linked to both Spanish and African cultures. These unique genres owe their rhythms to the drum. This instrument can be found in nearly every culture in the world.

Reread the first heading. **Underline** clues in paragraph 1 that show this is a good heading for the section.

COLLABORATE

Reread the second heading. Analyze how the author shows that both paragraphs are related. **Circle** what the author does to help you see that.

In paragraph 2, **draw a box** around the sentence that helps you understand the heading. How does the author support his choice for the heading? **Circle** the text evidence. Write it here:

1. _____

2. _____

3. _____

United in Sports

3   Even the sports we play have come from other places. Soccer's origins have been connected with a number of countries, including Italy and China. Tennis likely came from France, but some think it may have even been played in ancient Egypt. While no one may know the exact origin of some of these sports, there is no doubt they are now considered popular American activities.

4   Our nation has been enriched by a diversity of cultures. Learning the origins of what makes up American culture can lead to a new appreciation for the people and places from which they come.

Reread the excerpt. **Circle** two examples the author uses to support the heading of this section.

Talk with a partner about why "United in Sports" is a good heading. **Make a mark** in the margin beside the text evidence that supports your discussion.

Reread paragraph 4. **Underline** two benefits of diversity in our country. Write them here:

1. _____

2. _____
   _____

? **How do the headings help you understand the influence of other cultures on America?**

Talk About It Reread the headings on pages 28–29. With a partner, talk about how they are related and what the author wants you to understand.

Cite Text Evidence What text evidence shows that the headings and text are related? Write it in the chart.

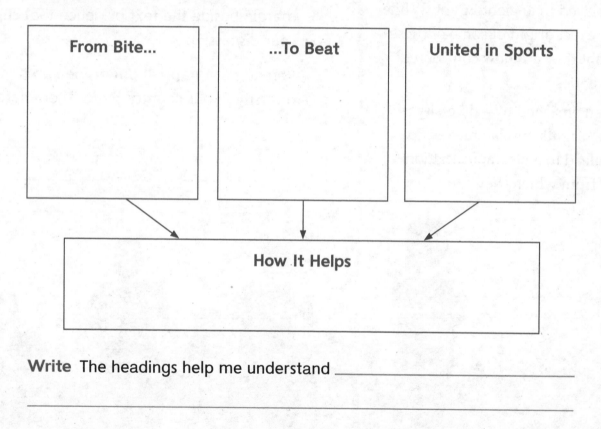

From Bite...	...To Beat	United in Sports

How It Helps

Write The headings help me understand _____

_____

_____

_____

Author's Purpose

An author has a purpose, or reason, for writing. When you read a text, think about what the author wants readers to know and why the author wants them to know this.

🔍 FIND TEXT EVIDENCE

Good writers do not use stereotypes. A stereotype is an oversimplified belief about a certain person, group, or issue. The purpose of stereotyping is to present a conventional image or opinion. The author of "Where Did That Come From?" tells about groups of people but stays away from stereotypes. Instead, the author tells how different groups have contributed to American culture. On page 28, the author uses the words "in fact" to correct stereotypes about some American dishes.

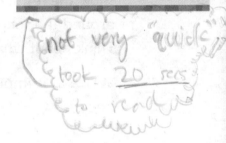

not very "quick" took 20 secs to read

> Dishes we think of as American have in fact come from all over the world. Hamburgers were crafted by German immigrants. Macaroni was rolled out by Italians.

Your Turn Reread paragraph 3 on page 29.

- What is the author's purpose? _The author's purpose is to inform us that sports comes from many different cultures created sports that we thought were American_

- How do you know this is the author's purpose? _He talked_

MAKE CONNECTIONS

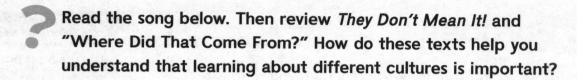

Read the song below. Then review *They Don't Mean It!* **and "Where Did That Come From?" How do these texts help you understand that learning about different cultures is important?**

COLLABORATE

Talk About It With a partner, read the song lyrics. Talk about why Frances Frost presents the song in two languages.

Cite Text Evidence **Circle** clues in the song that tell what the singer is doing. **Underline** details that show the result of the singer's actions. **Draw a box around** the songwriter's reason for taking action. Think about what the songwriter wants you to know.

Write It is important to learn about other cultures because _____

_____

_____

_____

_____

_____

_____

_____

De Lanterna na Mão
(With a Lantern in My Hand)

Eu procurei,
de lanterna na mão,
procurei, procurei, e achei
Você para o meu coração.
(repeat)

E agora, e agora
eu vou jogar
minha lanterna fora. (repeat)

I search for you with a lantern in my hand.
Searching here, searching there
and at last I find you, and you are my friend.
(repeat)

I have found you, I have found you
and now I can throw away my lantern.
(repeat)

— Frances Frost

CHECK IN 1 2 3 4

Write a Blog Entry

Think about the texts you read about experiencing different cultures. Why is it significant that people want to share their customs, traditions, and celebrations with others? Use text evidence to support your ideas.

1 Look at your Build Knowledge notes in your reader's notebook.

2 Write a blog entry about why it is significant that people want to share their customs, traditions, and celebrations with others.

3 Think about who will read your blog. Then think of examples from the texts that your readers will want to know about. Use new vocabulary words.

Think about what you learned in this text set. Fill in the bars on page 11.

Build Knowledge

What benefits come from people working as a group?

Build Vocabulary

Write new words you learned about what benefits come from working as a group. Draw lines and circles for the words you write.

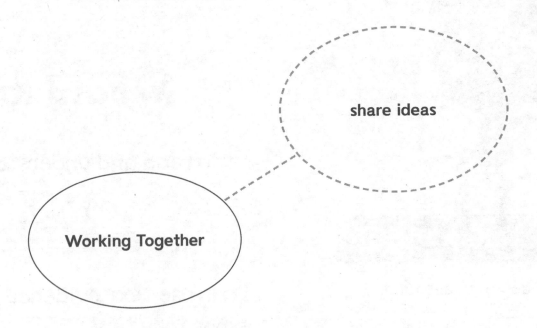

share ideas

Working Together

Go online to **my.mheducation.com** and read the "Two Heads Are Better than One" Blast. Think about working together. When do you work on your own and when is it better to work as part of a team? Then blast back your response.

Think about what you already know. Fill in the bars. It's okay if you want more practice.

Key

1 = I do not understand.

2 = I understand but need more practice.

3 = I understand.

4 = I understand and can teach someone.

What I Know Now

I can read and understand expository text.

I can use text evidence to respond to expository text.

1 2 3 4

I know what benefits come from working as a group.

STOP You will come back to the next page later.

> Think about what you learned.
> Fill in the bars. What progress did you make?

What I Learned

I can read and understand expository text.

1 2 3 4

I can use text evidence to respond to expository text.

1 2 3 4

I know what benefits come from working as a group.

1 2 3 4

My Goal I can read and understand expository text.

TAKE NOTES

Make note of interesting words and important information.

Gulf Spill Superheroes

Essential Question

?

What benefits come from people working as a group?

Read about how a variety of people worked together after the Deepwater Horizon oil spill in the Gulf of Mexico.

Joe Raedle/Getty Images News/Getty Images

Fans of comic books know that sometimes it takes a team of superheroes to save the day. Each one uses his or her special powers to fight an enemy or solve a problem. On April 20, 2010, the Deepwater Horizon drilling platform exploded in the Gulf of Mexico. Massive fires raged above the waters. Down below, gallons and gallons of oil spewed from a broken pipeline. Such a huge disaster would require the skills and abilities of many heroes working together.

Fire boats at work at the off shore oil rig Deepwater Horizon.

Responders in the Water

Immediately after the explosion, firefighters worked with the US Coast Guard to battle the blaze. Boats and aircraft transported survivors from the platform to safety before the rig sank.

Meanwhile, scientists raced to understand what was happening underwater. Each type of scientist had a specific **function.** Oceanographers mapped out the ocean floor and charted water currents in the area. Biologists looked for ways to protect animals in the region from the spreading oil.

What was most important, engineers discussed **techniques** to fix the broken well. The leak was more than a mile below the Gulf's surface. That was too deep for human divers to work effectively. For that reason, experts relied on robots with **artificial** arms and special tools to stop the spill. Many of their first efforts failed.

After nearly three months, workers finally plugged up the damaged well. It would take many more months to clean up the mess left behind.

◀ Workers move absorbent material to capture some spilled crude oil at Fourchon Beach, Louisiana.

(bkgd) Photodisc Collection/Getty Images; (tr) U.S. Coast Guard/Getty Images

FIND TEXT EVIDENCE

Read

Paragraph 1

Central Idea and Relevant Details

Look for details in paragraph 1. **Circle** the central, or main, idea in paragraph 1.

Paragraph 2

Latin Roots

The root *viv* means "to live." What is the meaning of *survivors* in paragraph 2?

_____

_____

Paragraphs 3-5

Ask and Answer Questions

How long did it take for the damaged well to be plugged up?

Reread

Author's Craft

How does the author use descriptive language to help you picture the effects of the accident?

Read

Paragraphs 1-2

Central Idea and Relevant Details

What is the central, or main, idea of "Watchers from the Sky"?

_____

_____

_____

Underline the text that supports the central idea.

Paragraphs 3-4

Ask and Answer Questions

Ask a question to check your understanding of "Heroes on Land."

_____

_____

Circle the answer to your question.

Reread

Author's Craft

How does the author help you understand the need for cooperation?

Watchers from the Sky

From the water, it was hard to see where the oil was spreading. Responders had to **collaborate** with other agencies, such as the NASA space program. Satellites in the sky sent information to scientists on the ground. Meteorologists tracked storms that might pose an **obstacle** to the response teams. Photographs helped team leaders decide how to assign their workers.

Pilots and their crews flew over the Gulf region in helicopters and planes. Some studied how the oil slick moved from place to place. Others directed the placement of floating barriers to protect sensitive areas. Some crews transferred needed supplies back and forth between land and sea.

Heroes on Land

As the oil approached land, new responders leapt into action. Veterinarians **dedicated** their efforts to helping out marine animals, such as pelicans and turtles. They would capture and treat affected animals before returning them to the wild. Naturalists and ecologists cleaned up the animals' habitats. Quite often, these groups' efforts overlapped, and they helped one another. Volunteers also helped out on many tasks.

Local fishermen also needed help. They relied on crabs, shrimp, and other seafood for their livelihood. Government officials monitored fishing areas to decide which were safe. Bankers and insurance companies also reached out to the fishermen. They helped find ways to make up for the lost income from seafood sales.

Biologists catch an oil-soaked brown pelican to clean and return to the wild.

Saul Loeb/AFP/Getty Images

In Florida, experts worked together in a "think tank." They needed to trap floating globs of oil before they ruined area beaches. They created the SWORD, or Shallow-water Weathered Oil Recovery Device. The SWORD was a catamaran with mesh bags hung between its two pontoons. The small craft would **mimic** a pool skimmer and scoop up oil as it moved. Because of its size and speed, the SWORD could be quite **flexible** responding to spills.

Workers place absorbent materials to catch oil in Orange Beach, Alabama.

As we have seen, the Deepwater Horizon accident required heroic efforts of all kinds. In some cases, workers' jobs were quite distinct. In others, their goals and efforts were similar. The success of such a huge mission depended on how well these heroes worked together. The lessons learned will be quite valuable if and when another disaster happens.

Summarize

Use the subheads and your notes to summarize important details about the Gulf oil spill. Then summarize the central idea of "Gulf Spill Superheroes."

EXPOSITORY TEXT

FIND TEXT EVIDENCE

Read

Paragraphs 1-2
Problem and Solution

Underline the problem mentioned in the first paragraph. How do the photo and caption work with the text to help you understand the solution to a problem?

_____

_____

_____

_____

_____

_____

_____

Reread

Author's Craft

Why does the author end the selection with "The lessons learned will be quite valuable if and when another disaster happens"?

Vocabulary

Use the example sentences to talk with a partner about each word. Then answer the questions.

artificial

Mike's **artificial** leg did not prevent him from playing most sports.

When might you want something to be artificial rather than real?

_____

_____

collaborate

Many students will **collaborate** to create our school's new banner.

What other projects might require you to collaborate with others?

_____

_____

dedicated

Tina **dedicated** herself to learning the song for the choir concert.

When have you dedicated all your efforts to learning something?

_____

_____

flexible

The dancer was so **flexible** that he could twist into almost any position.

Why is it important for athletes to be flexible?

_____

_____

function

The main **function** of a hammer is to pound nails.

What is the main function of another common tool?

_____

_____

 Build Your Word List Reread the third paragraph on page 40. Circle the word *responders*. In your reader's notebook, use a word web to write more forms of the word. For example, write *responsive*. Use an online or print dictionary to check for accuracy.

mimic

Some insects can **mimic** a twig to hide themselves.

What other animals can mimic something?

_____

_____

_____

obstacle

The fallen tree in the road was an **obstacle** for cars.

What sort of obstacle have you encountered trying to get somewhere?

_____

_____

_____

techniques

Maria uses a variety of bowing **techniques** when playing her violin.

What are some techniques you use to help you study?

_____

_____

Latin Roots

A root can be a clue to the meaning of an unfamiliar word. Some roots from ancient Latin are *sensus*, which means "perceive" or "feel"; *habitare*, which means "to live" or "to dwell"; and *port*, which means "carry." The prefix *trans-*, which means "across," also comes from ancient Latin.

🔍 FIND TEXT EVIDENCE

I know that the Latin root mare *means "the ocean or sea." Other context clues talk about how the oil spill affected life, so I can figure out that* marine *means "of or relating to the sea."*

> Veterinarians dedicated their efforts to helping out marine animals, such as pelicans and turtles.

Your Turn Use your knowledge of Latin roots to figure out the meanings of the following words from "Gulf Spill Superheroes":

transported, page 39 _____

sensitive, page 40 _____

habitats, page 40 _____

CHECK IN ▷ 1 ⟩ 2 ⟩ 3 ⟩ 4 ⟩

(l) Photodisc Collection/Eyewire/Getty Images; (r) Saul Loeb/AFP/Getty Images

Ask and Answer Questions

As you read an article, you may need to make adjustments when you do not understand some details. As you read "Gulf Spill Superheroes," you can stop, ask questions, and then look for answers. Asking and answering questions help you monitor, or check, your understanding of the article.

FIND TEXT EVIDENCE

When you read "Watchers from the Sky," you may get confused about how pilots and their crews helped. Ask, *Why would pilots and their crews be in charge of where to place floating barriers?* Reread to find the answer.

Page 40

Watchers from the Sky

From the water, it was hard to see where the oil was spreading. Responders had to **collaborate** with other agencies, such as the NASA space program. Satellites in the sky sent information to scientists on the ground. Meteorologists tracked storms that might pose an **obstacle** to the response teams. Photographs helped team leaders decide how to assign their workers.

Pilots and their crews flew over the Gulf region in helicopters and planes. Some studied how the oil slick moved from place to place. Others directed the placement of floating barriers to protect sensitive areas. Some crews transferred needed supplies back and forth between land and sea.

> **Quick Tip**
>
> You can annotate, or write a comment about, what you read to help you better understand the information. You can annotate in the margin of your own book, or you can use a sticky note in other books. Do not write in books that are not yours.

I reread the beginning of the section: From the water, it was hard to see where the oil was spreading. *People placing the floating barriers needed pilots above to see the oil, so pilots were in charge.*

Your Turn Ask and answer a question about the information in "Responders in the Water" on page 39. As you read, use the strategy Ask and Answer Questions.

_____

_____

_____

_____

CHECK IN 1 2 3 4

Problem and Solution

"Gulf Spill Superheroes" is expository text. Expository text gives factual information about a topic and may use a problem-and-solution text structure. The author may offer conclusions supported by evidence. Expository text may also include text features such as photographs, captions, and headings.

 FIND TEXT EVIDENCE

I can tell that "Gulf Spill Superheroes" is expository text about the Gulf Spill responders. The author uses a problem-and-solution text structure by telling the problem and describing solutions. Headings help organize the text. Photographs and captions provide additional information.

Page 40

Watchers from the Sky

From the water, it was hard to see where the oil was spreading. Responders had to **collaborate** with other agencies, such as the NASA space program. Satellites in the sky sent information to scientists on the ground. Meteorologists tracked storms that might pose an **obstacle** to the response teams. Photographs helped team leaders decide how to assign their workers.

Pilots and their crews flew over the Gulf region in helicopters and planes. Some studied how the oil slick moved from place to place. Others directed the placement of floating barriers to protect sensitive areas. Some crews transferred needed supplies back and forth between land and sea.

Heroes on Land

As the oil approached land, new responders leapt into action. Veterinarians **dedicated** their efforts to helping out marine animals, such as pelicans and turtles. They would capture and treat affected animals before returning them to the wild. Naturalists and ecologists cleaned up the animals' habitats. Quite often, these groups' efforts overlapped and they helped one another. Volunteers also helped out on many tasks.

Local fishermen also needed help. They relied on crabs, shrimp, and other seafood for their livelihood. Government officials monitored fishing areas to decide which were safe. Bankers and insurance companies also reached out to the fishermen. They helped find ways to make up for the lost income from seafood sales.

Biologists catch an oil-soaked brown pelican to clean and return to the wild.

Quick Tip

Text features can provide more information about the topic. Look at the photograph of the pelican covered in oil. It shows how serious the problem is and how important the solutions are. You should always read captions to gain more information.

Photographs and Captions

Photographs help to illustrate the information in the text. Captions provide additional information.

COLLABORATE **Your Turn** List an example of information that the author includes that shows problem-and-solution text structure. How do the photograph and caption on page 40 add details to the text?

_____

_____

_____

CHECK IN 1 2 3 4

Central Idea and Relevant Details

The **central idea** of an article is what it is mostly about. A central idea is supported by evidence, such as facts and **relevant details**. A central idea may be directly stated, but it is often implied. To find the central idea, identify relevant details to figure out what they have in common.

 FIND TEXT EVIDENCE

When I read "Heroes on Land," I can identify details such as the efforts of people on land working to help others. These details are relevant because they support a common idea. I can find the central idea.

Central Idea
As the oil spill reached land, other responders went to work.
Detail
Veterinarians and naturalists helped animals affected by the oil.
Detail
Business leaders helped fishermen who could not fish in some areas.
Detail
Members of a "think tank" created the SWORD to protect local beaches.

 Your Turn Reread "Responders in the Water" on page 39. Use the graphic organizer on page 47 to record text evidence about how responders helped to deal with the disaster.

> **Quick Tip**
>
> Each section and paragraph have a central idea. Also, headings can give a clue to the central, or main, idea. Find the relevant details that support the heading. Then determine what the details have in common.

CHECK IN ⟩ 1 ⟩ 2 ⟩ 3 ⟩ 4 ⟩

Central Idea
Detail
Detail
Detail

Respond to Reading

COLLABORATE

Discuss the prompt below. Use your notes and text evidence to write your response. Write a brief composition that answers the question below.

How might the outcome of the Deepwater Horizon accident have been different if fewer groups responded?

_____

_____

_____

_____

_____

_____

_____

_____

_____

_____

Quick Tip

Use these sentence starters to discuss the text.

- *Several groups were needed to . . .*

- *Teamwork was important because . . .*

- *Without so many groups, the outcome . . .*

Grammar Connections

Check that you have correctly punctuated compound sentences. A compound sentence contains two simple sentences joined together by a comma and a conjunction. For example, *They saw a problem, and they wanted to help.* Conjunctions include *and, but,* and *or.*

CHECK IN ⟩ 1 ⟩ 2 ⟩ 3 ⟩ 4 ⟩

Working Together

It takes a team of people to rescue animals and protect them from harm. Research one group that helps animals survive in their own ecosystems. Then create a television segment about that group. Work collaboratively with a larger group.

Step 1 | **Set a Goal** Generate questions you want to answer with research. Clarifying questions can help you understand confusing or complex ideas.

After you ask a clarifying question about your research on your topic, what would you do to find an answer?

_____

_____

_____

Step 2 | **Identify Sources** Use credible print or online sources. Websites that end in .gov or .edu are reputable and trustworthy. If you use websites that end in .org, make sure they are not biased.

Step 3 | **Find and Record Information** Take notes and cite your sources.

Step 4 | **Organize and Synthesize Information** Prepare for your segment. Plan the audio clips, photos, and videos you want to include.

Step 5 | **Create and Present** Think about how to present your segment. Members of your group will play the part of the rescue group to give information and answer questions. After your group completes your segment, you and your group will present it to the class.

Quick Tip

You can generate and clarify questions for formal inquiry or informal inquiry. Formal inquiry means using sources such as books, magazines, or websites to look for information. Informal inquiry means talking to people you know to get information.

Generate question:
- How does the group help animals?

Clarify question:
- Why do the animals need help?

What other clarifying question might you ask?

_____

_____

_____

CHECK IN 1 2 3 4

Winter's Tail

How do you know that the aquarium staff is concerned about Winter?

Literature Anthology: pages 198–211

Talk About It Reread paragraphs 2 and 3 on **Literature Anthology** page 202. Look at the photograph. Talk with a partner about how the staff helps Winter when she arrives at the aquarium.

Cite Text Evidence What evidence shows how the trainers feel about Winter? Write it in the chart.

Quick Tip

Focus on the details about the aquarium staff. Pay attention to descriptive words about their actions.

Text Evidence	Photograph Clues	What It Shows
The text says that the trainers carefully helped Winter and did their best to make her feel like she's home.	The photos show that	

Write I know that the aquarium staff is concerned about Winter because the authors _____

_____

_____

? **How do the authors help you visualize what the team had to think about while creating Winter's prosthesis?**

Talk About It Reread the last paragraph on **Literature Anthology** page 207. Turn to a partner and talk about what the team had to consider as they created the prosthesis.

Cite Text Evidence What words and phrases help you create a mental image of what the team did? Write text evidence in the chart.

Text Evidence	What I Visualize

Synthesize Information

How can looking up the definitions of unfamiliar science terms help you better visualize the text? Use an online source to find the definitions of *prosthesis* and *mimic*. Consider those definitions when visualizing the teams efforts.

Write I can visualize how the team created the prosthesis because the author _____

_____

? How do the authors show how Winter will continue to have an impact on the people who helped her?

COLLABORATE

Talk About It Reread the second paragraph on **Literature Anthology** page 211. Turn to a partner and discuss what the team will need to do.

Cite Text Evidence What does the team need to do in order to continue to help Winter? What is their goal? Write text evidence in the chart.

Text Evidence

↓

Text Evidence

↓

What I Know

Write I know that Winter will continue to be a part of her team's lives because _____

_____

_____

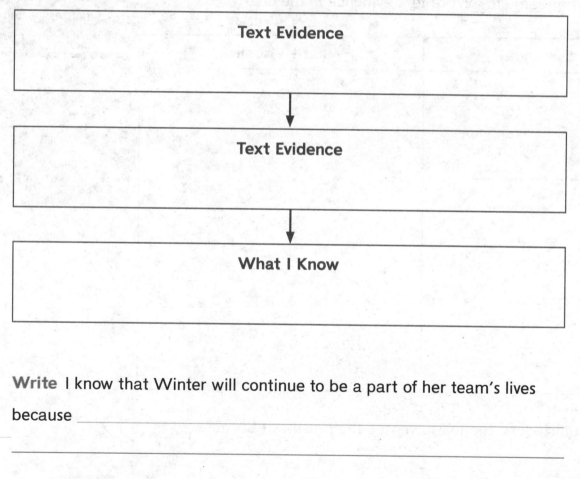

CHECK IN 1 2 3 4

Respond to Reading

COLLABORATE Discuss the prompt below. Use your notes and text evidence to support your answer. Make sure to write a response that is a paragraph long.

In what ways is Winter's story inspiring?

_____

_____

_____

_____

_____

_____

_____

_____

_____

_____

_____

_____

_____

_____

_____

_____

Quick Tip

Use these sentence starters to retell the selection and cite text evidence.

- *Without help from rescuers and aquarium staff . . .*

- *Winter's progress was . . .*

- *Winter inspired people by . . .*

CHECK IN ⟩ 1 ⟩ 2 ⟩ 3 ⟩ 4

Rene Frederic/age fotostock

Helping Hands

Literature Anthology:
pages 214-217

A Need Inspires

[1]   The rules of the competition asked participants to come up with new and innovative ways to help heal, repair or improve the human body. One of the group members, Kate Murray, understood the difficulties people with an injury or impairment can face. Kate was born with a left hand that was not fully formed. But that didn't stop Kate from taking part in activities. When she decided she wanted to learn how to play the violin, she and her mother worked with a team of specialists to create a device to allow her to hold a bow.

[2]   The Flying Monkeys wondered if they could create something similar for the competition. When one of their Girl Scouts coaches learned about Danielle Fairchild, a three-year-old who was born without fingers on her right hand, the Flying Monkeys found their inspiration.

Reread paragraph 1. **Underline** why Kate Murray understands how people with an injury or impairment feel.

Circle clues that help you understand what Kate is like.

COLLABORATE

Reread paragraph 2. Talk with a partner about how the Flying Monkeys found their inspiration. **Make a mark** in the margin beside the text evidence.

Why is "A Need Inspires" a good heading for this section? Use text evidence to write your answer here:

_____

_____

Introducing the BOB-1

1   Before long, the Flying Monkeys settled on a final design for their invention, which they called the BOB-1. They used a flexible plastic substance, a pencil grip, and hook-and-eye closures to build it. Everyone involved was impressed by how well the device would fit on Danielle's hand. What's more, it was very simple and inexpensive to make. Why hadn't anyone thought of creating a device like this before?

2   The Flying Monkeys created fliers, a portfolio, and even a skit to take to the competition and showcase their invention. The competition judges were impressed.

3   The Flying Monkeys won a regional and state-level innovation award. From there, it was on to the global round of the contest, where the BOB-1 would be judged alongside 178 other entries from 16 countries. The winning team would receive $20,000 to further develop the product.

In paragraph 1, **underline** how the author describes the BOB-1.

Reread paragraph 2. **Circle** what the group did to impress the judges at the competition. Write text evidence here:

1. _____

2. _____

3. _____

COLLABORATE

Reread paragraph 3. Talk about what happened at the competition and where the Flying Monkeys were headed next. **Draw a box** around how the author helps you understand the word *global*.

What remark does the author make about the Flying Monkeys' invention? Why does the author make this statement?

 Talk About It Look back at your text evidence and annotations on page 55. With a partner, talk about what remark the author makes about the Flying Monkeys' invention.

Cite Text Evidence How do you know what the author thinks about the Flying Monkeys' invention? Write text evidence in the chart.

What the Author Thinks About the Invention	

Write The author makes this statement to show _____

_____

_____

_____

CHECK IN 1 2 3 4

Literal and Figurative Language

To describe something, an author can use literal or figurative language. Literal language means exactly what it says. In figurative language, words are used in a different way from their usual meaning. Figurative language can be used to help readers better visualize something.

FIND TEXT EVIDENCE

In "Helping Hands" on **Literature Anthology** page 215, the author uses "cast aside" to describe what happened to "old ideas." The Flying Monkeys did not literally, or actually, throw an idea away. The author used "cast aside" to help readers visualize the process of finding an idea that works.

> Old ideas were cast aside and new ideas began to take shape.

Your Turn Reread paragraph 1 under "Introducing the BOB-1" on page 55.

- What descriptive words does the author use to help you visualize the device the Flying Monkeys invented? _____

_____

- Why do you think the author used literal instead of figurative language to describe the device? _____

_____

Think about the words you choose. Ask yourself whether literal or figurative language will be better to help readers visualize the meaning of your text. Here is an example of literal language: *The team was inspired to invent something.* Here is the same thought using figurative language: *Inspiration struck the team like lightning.*

CHECK IN 1 2 3 4

MAKE CONNECTIONS

? Look at the lithograph and think about the selections you read. Why is teamwork important?

Talk About It Look at the lithograph below. Read the caption. Talk with a partner about what the firefighters are doing.

Cite Text Evidence **Draw a box** around what the firefighters are battling. **Circle** the details that show how the firefighters are working together.

Write Teamwork is important because _____

_____

The Life of a Fireman: The New Era. Steam and Muscle was created in 1861 by American illustrator Charles Parsons. It was printed by Currier & Ives.

CHECK IN 1 2 3 4

Write a Speech

Think about the texts you read about people working together as a group. What qualities helped these groups succeed at their tasks? Use text evidence to support your ideas.

1 Look at your Build Knowledge notes in your reader's notebook.

2 Write a speech that explains the qualities that helped these groups succeed.

3 Use evidence from the texts you read. Briefly state how these groups successfully worked together and what impact they had. Use new vocabulary words.

Think about what you learned in this text set. Fill in the bars on page 37.

Build Knowledge

? Essential Question

How do we explain what happened in the past?

Build Vocabulary

Write new words you learned about how we can explain what happened in the past. Draw lines and circles for the words you write.

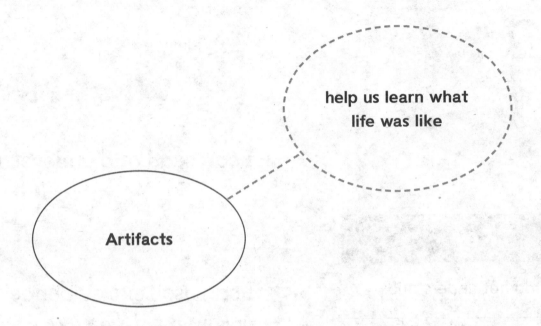

help us learn what life was like

Artifacts

Go online to **my.mheducation.com** and read the "Remnants of the Past" Blast. Think about the statues that were found. How does studying them help us learn about the past? Then blast back your response.

Think about what you already know. Fill in the bars. Let's keep learning!

What I Know Now

I can read and understand argumentative text.

1 > 2 > 3 > 4

I can use text evidence to respond to argumentative text.

1 > 2 > 3 > 4

I know how we can explain what happened in the past.

1 > 2 > 3 > 4

Key	
1 =	I do not understand.
2 =	I understand but need more practice.
3 =	I understand.
4 =	I understand and can teach someone.

 STOP You will come back to the next page later.

Think about what you learned. Fill in the bars. Keep working hard!

What I Learned

I can read and understand argumentative text.

| 1 | 2 | 3 | 4 |

I can use text evidence to respond to argumentative text.

| 1 | 2 | 3 | 4 |

I know how we can explain what happened in the past.

| 1 | 2 | 3 | 4 |

My Goal I can read and understand argumentative text.

TAKE NOTES

As you read, make note of interesting words and important information.

_____

_____

_____

_____

_____

_____

_____

_____

_____

_____

_____

_____

_____

TIME for **KiDS**

Essential Question

How do we explain what happened in the past?

Read two different views about the uses of a fascinating object.

The Inca Empire was centered in what is now Peru. It was taken by Spanish conquest in the middle of the 16th century.

SuperStock/Getty Images

What Was the Purpose of the Inca's
KNOTTED STRINGS?

String Theory

POINT / COUNTERPOINT

Was the quipu an ancient mathematical calculator?

Most of us do not do math problems without an electronic calculator. It would be even tougher without paper and pencil. Now imagine adding numbers with a device full of knotted strings! The quipu (pronounced KWEE-poo) was an invention of the Incas, an ancient civilization in South America. Most quipus were not **preserved**, but about 600 of them still remain **intact**.

Quipus are made of cotton and wool strings, sometimes hundreds of them, attached to a thicker horizontal cord. Both the **archaeologist** and the **historian** have tried to figure out how the quipu works. Here is their solution:

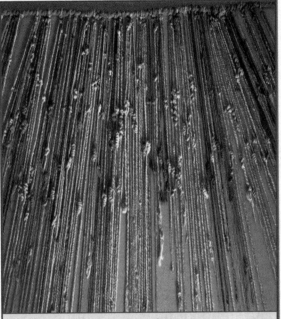

The quipu is an object that has baffled archaeologists for many years.

Knots were tied to the dangling strings to represent numbers.

The quipus were likely used by Inca officials to record and keep track of data, including statistics on anything from the number of crops produced by a village to the number of people living in a house.

Stuart Franklin/Magnum Photos

FIND TEXT EVIDENCE

Read

Paragraphs 1–2
Summarize

Underline an important idea you would use in a summary of the first two paragraphs. Write it here.

Paragraph 3
Context Clues

Circle the words that help you determine the meaning of *statistics*. Write the meaning here.

Make Inferences

Why might officials have wanted to record the number of crops and people in a village?

Reread

Author's Craft

Why does the author include the opening sentence?

(t) Neil Stewart; (b) STR/AP Images

FIND TEXT EVIDENCE

Read

Paragraphs 1–2

Author's Claim

Underline the sentence that states the first author's claim about the quipu. Discuss why a quipu was amazing.

_____

_____

Paragraphs 3–4

Summarize

What important idea would connect paragraphs three and four in a summary of "Spinning a Yarn"?

_____

_____

_____

_____

Reread

Author's Craft

Why does the author of "String Theory" include the illustration?

TIME for KiDS

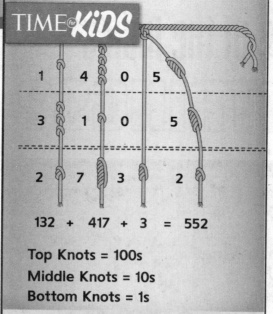

1	4	0	5
3	1	0	5
2	7	3	2

132 + 417 + 3 = 552

Top Knots = 100s
Middle Knots = 10s
Bottom Knots = 1s

Follow the illustration to understand how to count with a quipu.

Here is how a quipu would work: Each group of knots on a string represents a power of 10. Depending on their position, knots can stand for ones, tens, hundreds, and thousands. Clusters of knots increase in value the higher they are on the string. As a result, Incas with special training could add up the knots on a string to get the sum. They could also add up the total of many strings or even many quipus.

The patterns of the knots show repeating numbers. When you add it all up, it seems clear that the quipu was nothing less than an amazing low-tech calculator.

COUNTERPOINT Spinning a Yarn

The Incas had a 3D language written in thread!

Questions surround the Inca civilization. In its peak **era**—the middle of the 1400s—the Incas built thousands of miles of roads over mountains, and yet they didn't have wheeled vehicles. They made houses of stone blocks that fit together perfectly without mortar, a bonding material. The biggest question may be how the Incas kept their empire together without a written language.

The answer to the last question might be an odd-looking object called a quipu. Only a few hundred of these **remnants** of the Inca culture still exist.

Researchers discuss a quipu.

Quipus are made of wool strings that hang from a thick cord. On the strings are groups of knots. Many researchers believe the knots stand for numbers—even though no evidence supports this. But others make a strong case that the knots of the quipu were really language symbols, or a form of language.

Researchers found an identical three-knot pattern in the strings of seven different quipus. They think the order of the knots is code for the name of an Incan city. They hope to **reconstruct** the quipu code based on this and other repeating patterns of knots.

More conclusive proof that the quipu is a language comes from an old manuscript, a series of handwritten pages from the 17th century. It was found in a box holding **fragments** of a quipu. The author of the manuscript says the quipus were woven symbols. The manuscript even matches up the symbols to a list of words.

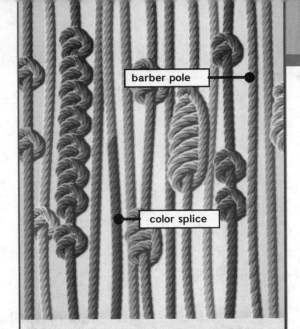
barber pole
color splice

Some experts now believe that the quipu's knots, colors, and patterns made it more than just a counting device. Decoding the quipu may reveal historical records.

The Inca empire covered nearly 3,000 miles. Perhaps the strings of the quipu helped hold it together.

Summarize

Use your notes and the illustrations to orally summarize important details and the central idea of each opinion text.

FIND TEXT EVIDENCE

> Read

Paragraphs 1–4
Author's Claim

Draw a box around the author's claim about quipus in the first paragraph.
Underline the evidence that supports this claim.

Diagrams

Circle information under the illustration that suggests an explanation for the quipu's knots. What does the illustration suggest?

_____

_____

_____

_____

_____

_____

> Reread

Author's Craft

How does the illustration support the author's claim?

Neil Stewart

Vocabulary

Use the example sentences to talk with a partner about each word. Then answer the questions.

archaeologist

An **archaeologist** looks for clues about ancient places and early cultures.

What ancient place would you visit if you were an archaeologist?

_____

_____

era

The people in the photograph wore clothes from an earlier **era**.

If you could time travel to a different era, which would you choose?

_____

_____

fragments

The vase was in **fragments** after it fell on the floor.

What fragments of objects have you found?

_____

_____

historian

A good **historian** finds interesting stories by studying past objects and events.

What would a future historian tell about the time you live in?

_____

_____

intact

Cardboard cartons help protect eggs and keep them **intact**.

What would you like to find intact after a storm?

_____

_____

Build Your Word List Pick a word you found interesting in the selection you read. Look up the definition in a print or online dictionary. Write the word and its definition in your reader's notebook.

preserved

We **preserved** food from our garden in jars.

Which of your possessions would you want preserved in a time capsule?

_____

_____

_____

reconstruct

We had to **reconstruct** our snow fort after it fell apart.

What things have you had to reconstruct?

_____

_____

_____

remnants

Divers discovered the **remnants** of a sunken ship.

What could someone learn from the remnants of a meal?

_____

_____

_____

Context Clues

When you come across an unfamiliar or multiple-meaning word, context clues found in the same sentence may help you determine its meaning. Sentence clues are words or phrases that help support the meaning of an unfamiliar word.

🔍 FIND TEXT EVIDENCE

In the first paragraph of "String Theory," I do not know the meaning of calculator. _The words_ do math problems _and_ electronic _in the sentence suggest that a calculator is a computer that solves math problems._

Most of us do not do math problems without an electronic calculator. It would be even tougher without paper and pencil.

Your Turn Use sentence clues to figure out the meanings of the following words from "String Theory" and "Spinning a Yarn."

patterns, _page 66_ _____

manuscript, _page 67_____

CHECK IN 1 2 3 4

Summarize

Summarizing argumentative texts as you read is a good way to keep track of how the authors make important points. Summarize sections as you read, and then summarize the whole text to check your understanding.

 FIND TEXT EVIDENCE

As you read "String Theory" on pages 65 and 66, summarize the author's theory of how the quipu might have been used.

Page 66

Here is how a quipu would work: Each group of knots on a string represents a power of 10. Depending on their position, knots can stand for ones, tens, hundreds, and thousands. Clusters of knots increase in value the higher they are on the string. As a result, Incas with special training could add up the knots on a string to get the sum. They could also add up the total of many strings or even many quipus.

The Incas' quipu had different patterns of knots on strings. Experts think the quipu may have been a calculator, and the patterns may have stood for numbers of different values.

 Your Turn Identify and summarize the claim in "Spinning a Yarn."

_____

_____

_____

CHECK IN 1 2 3 4

Compare and Contrast

An argumentative text tries to persuade an intended audience to agree with a claim supported with facts. You can **compare** and **contrast** two argumentative texts by seeing what is similar and different. For example, the authors of "String Theory" and "Spinning a Yarn" both think the quipu's knots have meaning, but each author has a different idea about that meaning. The texts also include diagrams that you can compare and contrast.

🔍 FIND TEXT EVIDENCE

I can tell that "String Theory" is argumentative text because it states a claim of how a quipu may have been used. Details about how the quipu worked support the claim. A diagram illustrates the information.

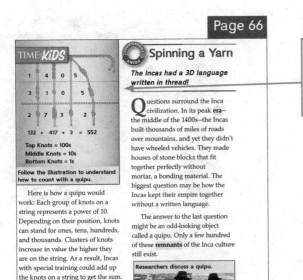

Page 66

Spinning a Yarn

The Incas had a 3D language written in thread!

Questions surround the Inca civilization. In its peak **era**—the middle of the 1400s—the Incas built thousands of miles of roads over mountains, and yet they didn't have wheeled vehicles. They made houses of stone blocks that fit together perfectly without mortar, a bonding material. The biggest question may be how the Incas kept their empire together without a written language.

The answer to the last question might be an odd-looking object called a quipu. Only a few hundred of these **remnants** of the Inca culture still exist.

Researchers discuss a quipu.

1 4 0 5
3 1 0 5
2 7 3 2
132 + 417 + 3 = 552

Top Knots = 100s
Middle Knots = 10s
Bottom Knots = 1s

Follow the illustration to understand how to count with a quipu.

Here is how a quipu would work: Each group of knots on a string represents a power of 10. Depending on their position, knots can stand for ones, tens, hundreds, and thousands. Clusters of knots increase in value the higher they are on the string. As a result, Incas with special training could add up the knots on a string to get the sum. They could also add up the total of many strings or even many quipus.

The patterns of the knots show repeating numbers. When you add it all up, it seems clear that the quipu was nothing less than an amazing low-tech calculator.

Diagram

A diagram is a simple visual representation of an object, place, idea, or event. Labels show how parts relate to one another and to the whole.

COLLABORATE

Your Turn How does the diagram on page 66 contrast with the diagram on page 67?

_____

_____

_____

_____

CHECK IN 1 2 3 4

Author's Claim

When an author of an argumentative text argues for or against an idea, the author is stating his or her **claim**. To identify the claim, look for reasons for or against an argument and then find evidence to support it. Details such as word choice, facts, and figures can help to develop the claim.

🔍 FIND TEXT EVIDENCE

I will look for reasons and evidence of the author's claim in "Spinning a Yarn." *Below the title is this sentence:* The Incas had a 3D language written in thread! *The author includes this reason to show a connection between the quipu and language. Then the author provides evidence to support this reason: that the knots were not counting devices but were language symbols.*

Details	Author's Claim
"Incas had a language in thread."	The author is in favor of quipu as a form of language.
knots may not mean numbers	
patterns may be symbols	
old manuscript shows a code	

Your Turn Identify important details in "String Theory" and place them in your graphic organizer on page 73. Then state the author's claim.

CHECK IN ▸ 1 ▸ 2 ▸ 3 ▸ 4

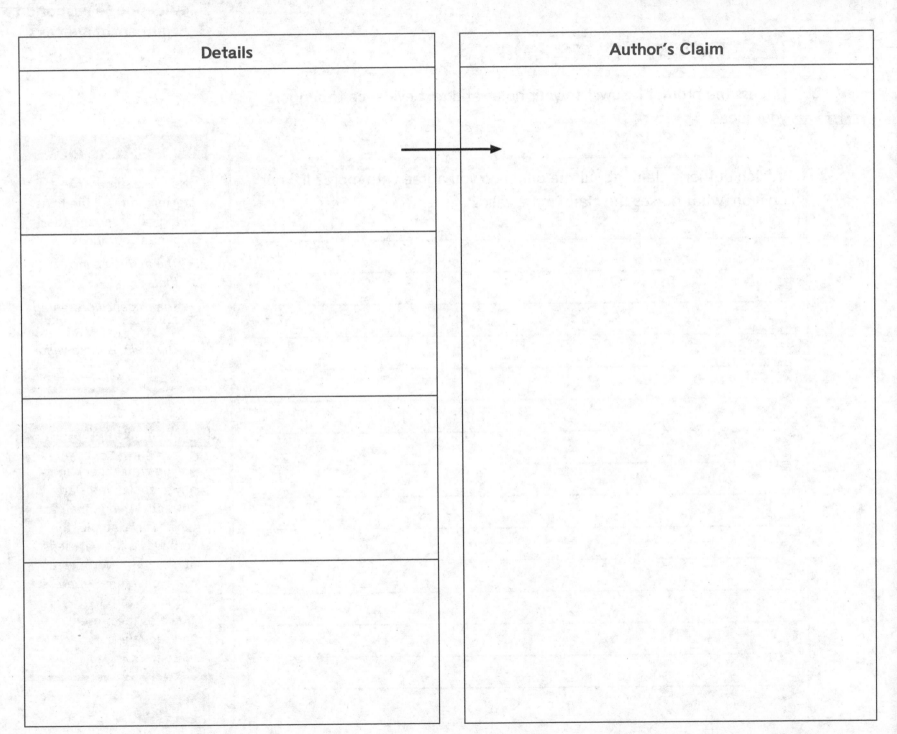

Details	Author's Claim

My Goal I can use text evidence to respond to argumentative text.

Respond to Reading

COLLABORATE

Discuss the prompt below. Use your notes and text evidence to support your ideas.

Which author's claim about the quipu do you agree with more? In your opinion, what makes the claim more valid?

_____

_____

_____

_____

_____

_____

_____

_____

_____

_____

_____

_____

_____

Quick Tip

Use these sentence starters to retell the texts in logical order and to organize your ideas.

- *The author claims that . . .*
- *The evidence presented includes . . .*
- *The claim is more valid because . . .*

Grammar Connections

As you write, check that any irregular verbs are correctly used in the past tense. For example, the verb *was* is the past tense of *is,* and the verb *were* is the past tense of *are. Think* is a verb that indicates the present, and *thought* is its past tense form.

CHECK IN ⟩ 1 ⟩ 2 ⟩ 3 ⟩ 4 ⟩

Investigating the Past

COLLABORATE

Ancestral Native American groups lived all over North America. Research the ancestors of one Native American group to create a multimedia presentation. Work collaboratively with a group.

Step 1 **Set a Goal** Generate questions about the ancestors of the Native American group you chose.

_____

Step 2 **Identify Sources** Think about how we know this information now. Which print sources or websites will your group use? How do you know that these are reliable sources?

_____

_____

Step 3 **Find and Record Information** Think about how text and audio features can enhance your presentation. For example, you might include photographs of sites where the people lived or recordings of someone speaking the language. As you find these features and other relevant information, take notes and cite your sources.

Step 4 **Organize and Synthesize Information** Organize your notes and draft your presentation. Select the text and audio features you wish to include.

Step 5 **Create and Present** Create your final presentation. Before sharing it with the class, review it. Is the display of your text features visible? Is the sound of your audio features clear?

The Ancestral Puebloans built and lived in large communities like these cliff dwellings. What does the photograph show that would be hard to describe in words?

_____

_____

> **Quick Tip**
>
> Additional text and audio features can include photographs of artifacts, captions, charts, graphs, illustrations, music, recorded speeches, or recorded sounds from events or places.

Tony Craddock/Shutterstock.com

CHECK IN ⟩ 1 ⟩ 2 ⟩ 3 ⟩ 4 ⟩

Machu Picchu: Ancient City

Literature Anthology: pages 218–221

 Why does the author address the claim that some experts believe Machu Picchu was an observatory?

 Talk About It Reread "The Royal Treatment" on **Literature Anthology** page 219. Turn to your partner and talk about what the author's perspective is and how the author supports this claim.

Cite Text Evidence How does the claim about the observatory relate to the author's perspective? Write text evidence in the chart.

 Make Inferences

Sometimes authors do not explain everything on the page. The author writes that archaeologists have tried to figure out why the Incas built Machu Picchu where it is. What inference can you make about Machu Picchu's location?

Author's Perspective

↓

Text Evidence

Write The author addresses the claim about the observatory because he or she wants to _____

_____

CHECK IN 1 › 2 › 3 › 4 ›

? **How does the author use literal language to help you visualize the Temple of the Sun?**

Talk About It Reread the fourth paragraph on **Literature Anthology** page 220. Turn to your partner and describe what the Temple of the Sun is like.

Cite Text Evidence What words and phrases help you visualize what the Temple of the Sun looks like? Write text evidence in the chart.

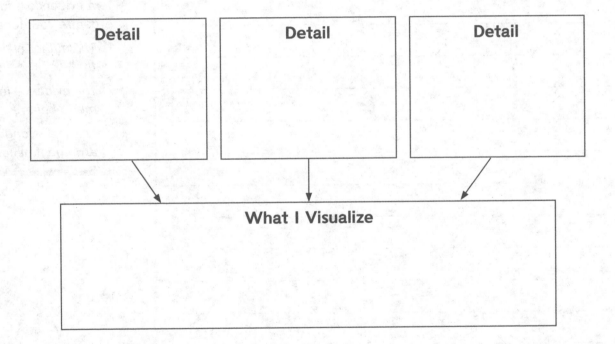

| Detail | Detail | Detail |

What I Visualize

Write The author uses literal language to help me visualize the Temple of the Sun by _____

_____

_____

_____

CHECK IN 1 2 3 4

Respond to Reading

COLLABORATE Discuss the prompt below. Use your notes and text evidence to support your answer.

What is your opinion about how ancient civilizations used Machu Picchu? Explain why you think your belief offers the stronger argument.

_____

_____

_____

_____

_____

_____

_____

_____

_____

_____

_____

_____

_____

_____

Quick Tip

Use these sentence starters to talk about the text evidence and to organize your ideas.

- *The author claims that . . .*

- *The evidence leads me to believe . . .*

- *This is a stronger argument because . . .*

CHECK IN ⟩ 1 ⟩ 2 ⟩ 3 ⟩ 4

Dig This Technology!

Literature Anthology:
pages 222–223

1   Another tool archaeologists use is a device that looks like a lawn mower. Called "ground penetrating radar" (GPR), it uses radar to locate artifacts under the ground. Radar bounces radio waves off an object to show its location. The diagram below shows how GPR helps archaeologists find artifacts.

Reread paragraph 1. **Circle** how the author describes the ground penetrating radar to help you understand what it looks like. **Underline** what the GPR does.

Look at the diagram. Talk with a partner about what the caption describes and what you see in the diagram. How does this help you understand more about what the GPR does? Use text evidence to write your response here:

_____

_____

_____

_____

_____

_____

Ground Penetrating Radar

One antenna sends radio waves into the ground. The other antenna receives waves when they bounce back. A wave that hits an object bounces back at a different depth than other waves. The depths are plotted on a display screen, revealing buried objects.

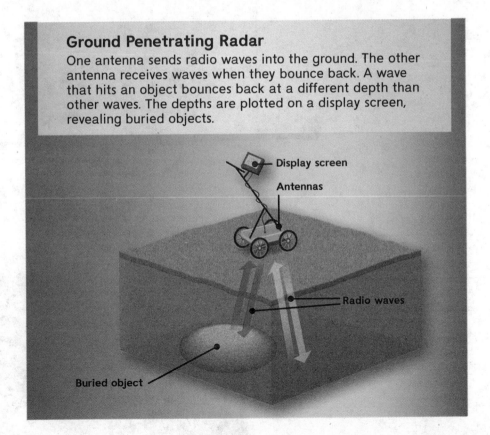

Display screen

Antennas

Radio waves

Buried object

? **How does the diagram help you understand how scientists find and analyze artifacts?**

Talk About It Reread the excerpt on page 79 and look at the diagram. With a partner, talk about what the diagram shows.

Cite Text Evidence What clues in the diagram help you understand how it helps scientists find and analyze buried artifacts? Write evidence in the chart.

Quick Tip

As you read each sentence in the caption, refer to the part of the diagram the sentence explains.

Evidence	How It Helps

Write The diagram helps me understand _____

_____

_____

_____

CHECK IN 1 2 3 4

Figurative Language

Writers use **figurative language** to help readers create mental images to deepen understanding or to make a strong point. Figurative language has a different meaning from the actual, literal, meaning of the words used.

 FIND TEXT EVIDENCE

In "Dig This Technology!" on page 223 of the **Literature Anthology,** the author creates a word picture to make a strong point about why new technology is helpful to archaeologists. The language used does not mean that archaeologists literally dig. It means they can look into the past with new ways today.

> Now, archaeologists can dig into the past without having to lift a shovel.

 Your Turn Read the following sentence:
Archaeologists use many different tools to carefully remove layers of dirt to find items people left in the ground long ago.

- Use figurative language to rewrite the sentence.

_____

_____

- Why did you choose to use this language?

_____

_____

Use figurative language in your writing to help readers create mental images of what you are describing. For example, if you want to describe the size of a large stone, you may write, "The stone was as big as an elephant." Using figurative language emphasizes important ideas or meaningful points you want to convey.

CHECK IN 1 2 3 4

? **How does the information in the photograph and the selections** *Machu Picchu: Ancient City* **and "Dig This Technology!" help you understand how we can explain what happened in the past?**

Talk About It Look at the photograph. Read the caption. Talk with a partner about what the paleontologist is doing.

Cite Text Evidence **Draw a box** around clues in the photo that show what Dr. Ross is doing. **Circle** some things he does to recreate the skeleton. In the caption, **underline** text evidence that explains what he is preparing the skeleton for.

Write The information helps me understand that

_____

_____

_____

_____

_____

_____

_____

_____

_____

_____

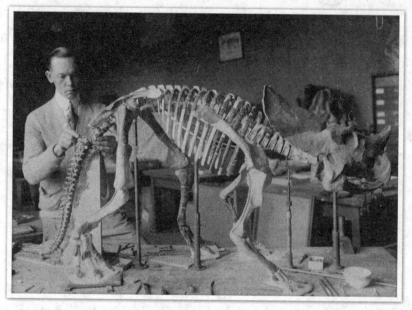

Norman Ross, a paleontologist, prepares a skeleton of a baby dinosaur for an exhibit. Ross worked at the National Museum in 1921.

CHECK IN 1 > 2 > 3 > 4

Write a Magazine Article

You read texts about studying the past. Think about why it is important to conduct research to figure out what happened in the past. How is research connected to why there might be more than one answer to explain what happened? Write a magazine article to answer this question. Use text evidence to support your ideas.

1 Look at your Build Knowledge notes in your reader's notebook.

2 Write your magazine article. Include a title and headings, if necessary.

3 Cite details and examples from the texts you read. Use new vocabulary words.

Think about what you learned in this text set. Fill in the bars on page 63.

Think about what you already know. Fill in the bars. It's important to keep learning.

What I Know Now

I can write an argumentative essay.

| 1 | 2 | 3 | 4 |

Key	
1 =	I do not understand.
2 =	I understand but need more practice.
3 =	I understand.
4 =	I understand and can teach someone.

I can synthesize information from three sources.

| 1 | 2 | 3 | 4 |

Think about what you learned.
Fill in the bars. What helped you do
your best?

What I Learned

I can write an argumentative essay.

1 > 2 > 3 > 4

I can synthesize information from
three sources.

1 > 2 > 3 > 4

WRITE TO SOURCES

You will answer an argumentative prompt using sources and a rubric.

ANALYZE THE RUBRIC

A rubric tells you what needs to be included in your writing.

Purpose, Focus, and Organization

Read the fourth bullet. Why should ideas be presented in a logical progression, or order?

Ideas _____

_____

_____

Evidence and Elaboration

Read the fourth bullet. What do you think precise language is?

_____

_____

_____

Evidence and Elaboration

Reread the fourth bullet. Why is it important to use precise language?

_____

_____

_____

Argumentative Writing Rubric

Purpose, Focus, and Organization • Score 4

- stays focused on the purpose, audience, and task
- makes a claim that clearly supports a perspective
- uses transitional strategies, such as words and phrases, to connect ideas
- presents ideas in a logical progression, or order
- begins with a strong introduction and ends with a strong conclusion

Evidence and Elaboration • Score 4

- effectively supports the claim with logical reasons
- has strong examples of relevant evidence, or supporting details, from multiple sources
- uses elaborative techniques, such as examples, definitions, and quotations from sources
- **expresses interesting ideas clearly using precise language**
- uses appropriate academic and domain-specific language
- uses different sentence structures

Turn to page 236 for the complete Argumentative Writing Rubric.

Precise Language

Express Ideas Clearly Writing should be coherent, or easy to follow. Using precise language means using the exact right words. Precise language helps writers express their ideas clearly in an argumentative essay. It also improves sentence structure and helps readers follow ideas in a sentence. Read the paragraph below. Examples of precise language are highlighted.

> The quipu, an **invention** of the Incas, was perhaps used by the Incas in the Inca Empire to **keep track of** data. The quipu has strings and knots, and the strings and knots were likely a representation of data used by the Incas. Some archaeologists believe the Incas used the quipu to perhaps keep track of crops grown in the Inca Empire.

The exact word *invention* helps readers understand what a quipu is. The words *keep track of* tell exactly what a quipu does.

Delete Unnecessary Ideas To improve sentence structures, writers do not repeat words and phrases in the same sentence. They also avoid using words with similar meanings in the same sentence. Reread the paragraph above. Revise it by crossing out unnecessary words.

Purpose

Good writers consider not only what they want to write, but how they write it. They consider their purpose for writing in order to choose the most precise language. Precise language helps the reader visualize the details in an argument. The ideas in a precisely worded argument also set a more formal tone.

ANALYZE THE STUDENT MODEL

Paragraph 1

Read the first paragraph of Joe's essay. Examples of precise language are highlighted.

What is Joe's argument?

_____

_____

_____

_____

Paragraph 2

List examples of transitional words or phrases that connect ideas.

_____

_____

Paragraph 2

Circle an example of precise language. How does this example support Joe's argument?

_____

_____

_____

_____

Student Model: Argumentative Essay

Joe responded to the Writing Prompt: _Write an argumentative essay to present to your class. Answer the question: What is the best way to learn a language—in a class setting or from online learning?_ Read Joe's essay below.

1　　There's no doubt that learning a language is a good thing. However, my opinion is that the best way to learn a language is in a **classroom**, immersed with other students. In **immersion** classrooms, students learn more than the language, and they become prepared for the **future**.

2　　Learning another language in a classroom offers students a broader range of studies. The article "Language Classes" says that in an immersion class, "students are taught a number of subjects in both languages." In other words, students are learning a language in other subjects. "Language Classes" also describes a program called Foreign Language in Elementary schools, or FLES. In FLES, the foreign language instruction is connected to science, technology, engineering, arts, and math. Nancy Rhodes, an education official, reports that classroom immersion is the best way to get results. The article "Language Classes" also describes a class where students learned Chinese and studied Chinese culture, including about the country's climate, plants, and animals. They cooked Chinese food and did martial arts. Classrooms like this make learning a language immediately applicable. For example, if I were in a French immersion class, I could learn French grammar but also write a science lab report in French. And maybe even cook French food and speak in French while my classmates enjoy the meal. Those aren't activities students can do online!

3   Learning in a classroom provides interactions with real people, which helps students prepare for jobs later on. The benefits of practicing another language with real people can be huge, especially after students graduate and look for work. In fact, according to "Why Learn Languages?" the American Council on the Teaching of Foreign Language finds that schools with language classes help different cultural groups get along. People aren't interacting with digital voices or videos. People are interacting with real people! Consider that French immersion class again. I would have authentic conversations and cover many topics. As a result, my understanding would be well-rounded and better fit into daily life now and in the future.

4   I did read in "Online Language Learning" that some online programs offer ways to interact socially with other users or with teachers. However, students experience most online learning alone. In classrooms, everyone can practice and improve together. The best learning happens face-to-face, with others who want the same knowledge.

ARGUMENTATIVE ESSAY

Paragraph 3

Joe supports his argument with an example in paragraph 3. **Underline** this example.

How does this example support his argument?

_____

_____

_____

_____

Paragraph 4

Draw a box around the source that Joe includes to support his argument.

Paragraph 4

Reread the conclusion. What example of precise language does Joe use in his conclusion? Underline it.

Apply the Rubric

With a partner, use the rubric on page 86 to discuss why Joe scored a 4 on his essay.

> **My Goal** I can write an argumentative essay.

Analyze the Prompt

Writing Prompt

Write an argumentative essay to present to your class: Answer the question: Should students participate in study abroad programs?

Purpose, Audience, and Task Reread the writing prompt. What is your purpose for writing? My purpose is to _____

_____

Who will your audience be? My audience will be _____

_____

What type of writing is the prompt asking for? _____

_____

Set a Purpose for Reading Sources Asking questions about whether students should participate in study abroad programs will help you figure out your purpose for reading. It also helps you understand what you already know about the topic. Before you read the passage set about study abroad programs, write a question here.

_____

_____

_____

_____

Fstop/ImageSource

Read the following passage set.

PARENTS SAY NO TO STUDY ABROAD

1   Parents must consider many factors before allowing their children to study in another country. Because of the requirements, costs, and risks, parents should say no to study abroad.

2   One concern for parents is the **paperwork**. Most students will need a passport and a visa. A visa is a **document** that gives students **permission** to study and live in the country. Students must **apply** for a visa and prove their enrollment, funding, and housing. Students may also need **international** medical insurance, shots, and medications to ensure their health needs are met. Although parents can work with the school to gather information and prepare documents, not all parents and schools have the resources to do so.

3   The second concern is the cost. Traveling to and living in another country for weeks or months can cost more than living and studying at home. Flights, transportation, food, lodging, and tuition can add up. One semester in England, for example, could cost as much as $7,000. Even a less expensive destination could be $4,000 per semester. Consider communication costs, like cell phone service and Internet. There's also the exchange rate. The US dollar is sometimes worth less in other countries, making everyday items expensive.

4   Lastly, parents fear for their children's safety. Even if students travel to safe places, some parents worry that their children will struggle without the comforts, structure, and familiarity of home. A chaperone may be a poor substitute for a knowledgeable parent.

ARGUMENTATIVE ESSAY

FIND TEXT EVIDENCE

Paragraph 1
Underline the claim.

Paragraph 2
Read the highlighted examples of precise language.

How do these examples of precise language make the author's argument more credible?

_____

_____

_____

_____

_____

_____

Paragraphs 2–4
Circle the transitional word or phrase in each paragraph that signals the order of reasons listed in paragraph 1.

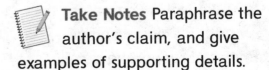 **Take Notes** Paraphrase the author's claim, and give examples of supporting details.

WRITING

FIND TEXT EVIDENCE

Paragraphs 5–6

Read the highlighted examples of precise language.

How do these examples of precise language support the argument?

_____

_____

_____

Paragraph 7

Circle examples of transitional words and phrases in this paragraph.

Paragraph 8

Underline the transitional phrase that introduces a supporting detail.

Paragraph 9

Draw a box around the closing statement.

Take Notes Paraphrase the author's claim, and give examples of supporting details.

SOURCE 2

The Benefits of Study Abroad Programs

5   Today, students participate in study abroad programs all over the world. When students live abroad and study foreign languages, they **experience** many benefits. They **expand** their **worldview**, they become more **empathetic** to others, and they are more likely to have **significant advantages** in their **careers** later in life.

6   Firstly, students experience the world differently when they are fluent in a foreign language. They join in daily traditions and customs, such as buying produce at farmers' markets. Speaking fluently with the locals gives students a rare enriching experience. Students thus acquire a cross-cultural awareness.

7   Secondly, students who study a foreign language have greater empathy for others. When comprehending another language, students consider other people's perspectives. This enables them to better understand not only the words people say but also the feelings people express. Studies show that this exposure to other languages instills a deeper awareness of speakers' intentions.

8   Finally, learning a foreign language is critical in today's workforce. Many jobs in education or business favor bilingual candidates. For example, companies with international clients require bilingual candidates. Students who study abroad and speak another language are attractive to future employers.

9   Learning a foreign language during study abroad has benefits that outweigh the many costs and paperwork. It bridges perspectives. It influences the way people view the world, not just their local communities. Above all, it deepens cultural understanding and promotes communication.

US Students STUDY ABROAD

10   The number of American students studying abroad has greatly increased, thanks to smarter decisions about costs and time.

11   Since 2000, trends have shown to be mostly consistent. The US recession in 2008 did slow the number of students studying abroad. But students and their families have made smarter decisions about study abroad as the US economy bounced back.

12   In fact, research shows that students are still choosing to study abroad in increasing numbers. However, they are studying abroad for shorter periods of time and living in countries with more affordable costs. They are also choosing to learn languages in countries that have growing businesses. That demand requires more people globally to speak the language.

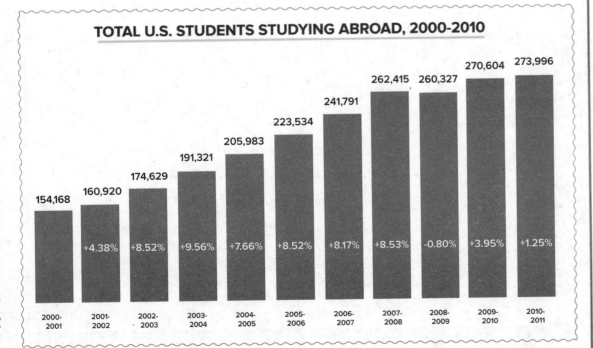

TOTAL U.S. STUDENTS STUDYING ABROAD, 2000-2010

Year	Students	Change
2000-2001	154,168	
2001-2002	160,920	+4.38%
2002-2003	174,629	+8.52%
2003-2004	191,321	+9.56%
2004-2005	205,983	+7.66%
2005-2006	223,534	+8.52%
2006-2007	241,791	+8.17%
2007-2008	262,415	+8.53%
2008-2009	260,327	-0.80%
2009-2010	270,604	+3.95%
2010-2011	273,996	+1.25%

(t)ibrandify gallery/Shutterstock; (chart)McGraw-Hill Education

---

ARGUMENTATIVE ESSAY

FIND TEXT EVIDENCE

Paragraph 10
Draw a box around the author's claim.

Paragraphs 11–12
Underline the words that tell how American families solved the problem of study abroad costs.

Paragraph 12
Circle the transitional words in this paragraph.

Study Abroad Infographic
What do you notice about the number of students studying abroad every year since 2000?

_____

_____

_____

_____

Take Notes Paraphrase the author's claim, and give examples of supporting details.

My Goal I can synthesize information from three sources.

TAKE NOTES

Read the writing prompt below. Write your claim. Then use the three sources, your notes, and the graphic organizer to plan a response.

Writing Prompt *Write an argumentative essay to present to your class. Answer the question: Should students participate in study abroad programs?*

Synthesize Information

Review the evidence recorded from each source. What does the evidence tell you about whether students should study abroad or not? Discuss your ideas with a partner.

CHECK IN ⟩ 1 ⟩ 2 ⟩ 3 ⟩ 4 ⟩

Plan: Organize Ideas

Claim	Reasons
Study abroad programs are . . .	One reason that students should consider . . .

Relevant Evidence

Source 1	Source 2	Source 3

(bkgd) Valentain Jevee/Shutterstock

Draft: Logical Order

Organize Ideas Logically Writers of argumentative essays want to convince an audience, so they carefully structure their evidence. Evidence should be organized and presented in a logical order. Writers may choose to put their strongest reason either first or last, where it will stand out the most. In the example below from "What Was the Purpose of the Inca's Knotted Strings?" the author introduces a claim with a strong fact about the quipu.

> More conclusive proof that the quipu is a language comes from an old manuscript, a series of handwritten pages from the 17th century. It was found in a box holding fragments of a quipu. The author of the manuscript says the quipus were woven symbols. The manuscript even matches up the symbols to a list of words.

Now use the above paragraph as a model to write one claim. In the first sentence, try to use a strong reason to introduce the claim.

_____

_____

_____

 Draft Use your graphic organizer and the example above to write your draft in your writer's notebook. Before you start writing, review the rubric on page 86. Remember to indent each paragraph. Also, make sure to use transitional words that signal a logical order. For example, the words *first, second, lastly,* or *finally* indicate sequence.

Grammar Connections

A pronoun takes the place of one or more nouns. A pronoun must match the number and gender of its antecedent, which is the noun (or nouns) to which it refers. In the example on the left, "It" matches the number and gender of the antecedent, "manuscript."

CHECK IN 1 2 3 4

Revise: Peer Conferences

COLLABORATE

Review a Draft Listen actively to your partner. Take notes about what you liked and what was difficult to follow. Begin by telling what you liked. Use these sentence starters.

Your transitional words helped me understand . . .
This word is a great example of precise language because . . .
What do you mean by this detail . . .

After you finish giving each other feedback, reflect on the peer conference. What suggestion did you find to be the most helpful?

_____

_____

_____

Revision Use the Revising Checklist to help you figure out what text you may need to move, elaborate on, or delete. After you finish writing your final draft, use the full rubric on pages 236–239 to score your essay.

✔ Revising Checklist

- ☐ Did I use precise language to express my ideas clearly?
- ☐ Did I support my argument with strong relevant evidence?
- ☐ Did I present my evidence logically? Did I use transitions?
- ☐ Are the ideas in my introduction and conclusion connected?
- ☐ Did I check my spelling and punctuation?

Next, you'll write an argumentative essay on a new topic.

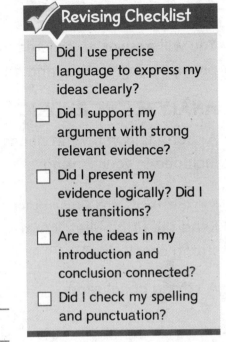

My Score			
Purpose, Focus, & Organization (4 pts)	Evidence & Elaboration (4 pts)	Conventions (2 pts)	Total (10 pts)

WRITE TO SOURCES

You will answer an argumentative prompt using sources and a rubric.

ANALYZE THE RUBRIC

A rubric tells you what needs to be included in your writing.

Purpose, Focus, and Organization
Read the fifth bullet. What is a strong conclusion?

A strong conclusion _____

_____

_____

Evidence and Elaboration
Read the third bullet. What does the word "elaborative" mean?

_____

_____

Evidence and Elaboration
Read the fourth and sixth bullets. What is the connection between expressing ideas clearly and using different sentence structures?

_____

_____

_____

Argumentative Writing Rubric

Purpose, Focus, and Organization • Score 4
• stays focused on the purpose, audience, and task
• makes a claim that clearly supports a perspective
• uses transitional strategies, such as words and phrases, to connect ideas
• presents ideas in a logical progression, or order
• **begins with a strong introduction and ends with a strong conclusion**

Evidence and Elaboration • Score 4
• effectively supports the claim with logical reasons
• has strong examples of relevant evidence, or supporting details, from multiple sources
• uses elaborative techniques, such as examples, definitions, and quotations from sources
• expresses interesting ideas clearly using precise language
• uses appropriate academic and domain-specific language
• uses different sentence structures

Turn to page 236 for the complete Argumentative Writing Rubric.

Valentain Jevee/Shutterstock

Strong Conclusion

End With a Strong Statement In an argumentative essay, it is especially important to end with a strong conclusion, which is a paragraph at the end of a text that summarizes the most important idea and details. The goal is to leave the reader thinking about the author's ideas and agreeing with the author's argument.

Read the sample conclusion below. The author concludes with a strong statement that clearly states his or her perspective about forests and what must be done to save them.

> Nations **should** not wait for a disaster to happen. We **must** look beyond local needs. They **must** adopt a global perspective. We **need** to preserve forests for the benefit of all.

Strong Language Reread the sample conclusion above. Notice that the words *should, must,* and *need* are highlighted. These are examples of strong words that clearly communicate the author's argument.

Now use the paragraph above as a model to draft a conclusion you might use to write an argumentative essay about Machu Picchu. Make sure to use examples of strong language.

_____

_____

_____

_____

Audience

Good writers think about their audience when they make an argument. They choose to use either a formal or informal tone and consistently use it throughout their writing. If you want to use a more serious tone, use *believe* instead of *think* and use *assert* instead of *say*. These two words *believe* and *assert* are examples of academic language that gives your writing a more formal tone.

ANALYZE THE STUDENT MODEL

Paragraph 1

Underline Suze's claim. What is a detail from her introduction that caught your attention?

_____

_____

_____

Paragraph 2

Circle the detail that tells you the anthropologist is a reliable source of information. How does this source support Suze's argument?

_____

_____

_____

Paragraph 3

Draw a box around the transitional words Suze uses in the beginning of the third paragraph.

Student Model: Argumentative Essay

Suze responded to the Writing Prompt: *Write an article for a bulletin board display stating your argument about who created Costa Rica's stone spheres.* Read Suze's essay below.

1 Who made the mysterious stone spheres in Costa Rica? One theory says that they may have been shaped by erosion over thousands of years. Another theory claims that they were brought here by aliens from outer space! However, most scientists and archaeologists agree that the spheres were made by the ancient Diquis people.

2 In the 1930s, a fruit company discovered the spheres when they began clearing land near a river. According to the article "Stone Spheres of Costa Rica," there are about three hundred of them in existence. The largest weighs 16 tons. An anthropology professor, a leading expert on the Costa Rican spheres, says the spheres were made by the Diquis people. He noticed marks on the spheres from stone hammers. Grinding and sanding were also used to help shape the spheres. The professor said that making the spheres "was accomplished without the help of metal tools, laser beams, or alien life-forms."

3 Some people think that the spheres may have been shaped by nature. In the article "Made by Nature," the

author compares the spheres to the giant stone spheres in Jalisco, Mexico. The Mexican spheres were shaped by volcanic eruptions and erosion. Since the Costa Rican stone spheres were found near the Diquis River, the theory is that water erosion may have shaped them. However, the spheres are perfectly smooth, unlike the ones in Mexico that have rough surfaces.

4   Because the stone spheres are so smooth, one theory is that extraterrestrials brought them. According to the travel blog "Out of This World," an ancient civilization couldn't have carved the stone spheres. They are too big and perfectly round to have been made without modern tools. I can tell the blog isn't a reliable source. The author is not a scientist, and most importantly, no facts or evidence are included to support the author's theory.

5   The stone spheres of Costa Rica are still a mystery in some ways. For example, why did the Diquis people create these mammoth spheres? What we do know is that the spheres were not sculpted by water or a volcanic eruption. Nor were they delivered by aliens from outer space! The spheres were created with stone tools by an ancient civilization in Costa Rica.

ARGUMENTATIVE ESSAY

Paragraph 3
What text structure does Suze use in this paragraph?

_____

_____

Paragraph 4
Circle the source used in paragraph 4. **Underline** details that tells you why it is not a reliable source.

Paragraph 5
Underline a strong statement. Read the highlighted sentence. What idea does this restate from the introduction?

_____

_____

_____

_____

Apply the Rubric

With a partner, use the rubric on page 98 to discuss why Suze scored a 4 on her essay.

Analyze the Prompt

Writing Prompt

Write an argumentative essay to present to your class. Answer the question: Why is it important to treat archaeological sites with respect?

Purpose, Audience, and Task Reread the writing prompt. What is your purpose for writing? My purpose is to _____

_____

Who will your audience be? My audience will be _____

_____

What type of writing is the prompt asking for? _____

_____

Set a Purpose for Reading Sources Asking questions about why it is important to treat archaeological sites with respect will help you figure out your purpose for reading. It also helps you understand what you already know about the topic. Before you read the passage set about archaeological sites write a question here.

_____

_____

_____

REMEMBER
St. Helena's Role

1 During the nineteenth century, over three million Africans were enslaved and transported from West Africa to the West Indies. This voyage was called the Middle Passage. It was part of a triangular trade route linking Europe, Africa, the West Indies, and the British Colonies.

2 Since 1807, Royal Navy ships patrolled the Atlantic Ocean, capturing slave ships. From 1840 to 1872, the Royal Navy brought 25,000 freed slaves to St. Helena, an island about 1,000 miles off southwest Africa's coast. A camp and hospital were located there. Almost eight thousand of the freed Africans died there. They were sick because of the terrible conditions on the slave ships.

3 In 2008, archaeologists excavated a site in St. Helena that contained 325 bodies. One-third of the skeletons were children, age twelve years or younger. Only seventeen people were aged thirty-six to forty-five, and they were the oldest. Archaeologists were unable to determine the exact cause of death, but the brutality of enslavement was clear.

4 In the graves, archaeologists recovered some metal bracelets and glass beads from necklaces. For the Africans, these objects from their homeland must have been extraordinarily important.

5 The St. Helena site is **unique**. It contains first-generation Africans who were taken directly from the slave ships, only a few weeks away from their homeland. It gives a **human** face to the **horrors** of the Middle Passage and a place where we can and **must commemorate** the dead.

ARGUMENTATIVE ESSAY

FIND TEXT EVIDENCE 🔍

Paragraphs 1–2
Underline the details that describe how many Africans were affected by the Middle Passage. How many freed slaves were brought to St. Helena?

_____

Paragraph 4
Circle the details that tell what the author concludes about the objects.

Paragraph 5
Read the highlighted words. How does the author feel about the St. Helena site?

_____

_____

_____

Take Notes Paraphrase the author's claim and give examples of supporting details.

FIND TEXT EVIDENCE

Paragraphs 6–7

Draw a box around the details that tell you what the Angel Mounds site is comprised of. Why is the site important?

_____

_____

_____

Paragraph 8

Underline why Thompson's elders approved of her working at Angel Mounds. What are the Native Americans protecting?

_____

_____

Paragraph 9

Read the highlighted examples of strong language in paragraph 9. **Circle** the statement that expresses the author's perspective about Native American sites.

 Take Notes Paraphrase the author's claim, and give examples of supporting details.

SOURCE 2

Collaboration at
ANGEL MOUNDS

6   Angel Mounds is a Native American site in southwest Indiana. It is one of the best-preserved archaeological sites in North America. It is also an example of collaboration between archaeologists and tribes who are the descendants of the people who made the site, says Ashleigh Thompson. She is a member of the Red Lake Band of Ojibwe and a college-level archaeologist working at Angel Mounds.

7   The site contains four large platform mounds, smaller earthen mounds, and hundreds of structures. About one thousand people once lived there. They are descended from the Mississippian culture. The Mississippian people lived from about 800 C.E. to 1600 C.E. They are known as mound-builders.

8   When Thompson chose to work at Angel Mounds, her elders approved. They believed that a Native American archaeologist would protect their artifacts and remains. However, Thompson points out that many archaeologists do collaborate with tribes. They ask permission to research Native American sites. They follow laws that help tribes protect their ancestors' graves. In fact, she remembers when her lead archaeologist listened to Native Americans' concerns about the human remains and respected their wish to bury them.

9   Thompson **asserts** that **cooperation** between archaeologists and tribes ensures that both parties are heard and helps everyone learn. A **successful collaboration** at Angel Mounds can be a model for other Native American archaeological sites. It shows that people can work together and keep their values intact.

No Digging Allowed

10   Throughout history, archaeologists have disrupted many Native American sites. They studied sites without asking Native Americans' permission. They took artifacts to study or donate to museums. They dug up graves and took Native Americans' ancestors' human remains.

11   What these archaeologists did has made many Native Americans upset. According to Native American tribal teachings, their ancestors shouldn't be disturbed. To restore this balance, they requested that museums return their ancestors' remains and artifacts. They protested and wrote letters to elected officials. Their requests were mostly ignored.

12   After much convincing, Congress passed the Native American Graves Protection and Repatriation Act in 1990. As a result, museums have returned much of what they took.

13   But many Native Americans lost part of their living culture when their artifacts were taken. They believe that their life journey isn't complete until their human remains reside in the earth where they once lived. In August 2007, Apache artifacts were returned to Arizona in shipping crates with breathing holes for the artifacts inside. Apache leaders buried them in sacred sites where they believe the spirits live.

14   Today, it is illegal to buy and sell Native American artifacts. But it may also be a crime to remove them from the dirt, bottoms of rivers, or anywhere else, however unknowingly. Native American tribal members believe that sites shouldn't be disturbed at all. Now the law is on their side.

FIND TEXT EVIDENCE

Paragraph 10

Underline the claim. What do the supporting details tell you about how archaeologists felt about Native American beliefs?

_____

_____

_____

Paragraph 11

Circle the ways Native Americans made their perspectives known.

Paragraphs 12–13

What effect did the Native American Graves Protection and Repatriation Act have?

_____

_____

_____

Paragraph 14

Draw a box around what Native Americans believe.

Take Notes Paraphrase the author's claim and give examples of supporting details.

WRITING

My Goal I can synthesize information from three sources.

TAKE NOTES

Read the writing prompt below. Write your claim. Then use the three sources, your notes, and the graphic organizer to plan a response.

Writing Prompt *Write an argumentative essay to present to your class. Answer the question: Why is it important to treat archaeological sites with respect?*

Synthesize Information

Review the evidence recorded from each source. How does the information show why archaelogical sites should be treated with respect? Discuss your ideas with a partner.

CHECK IN 1 2 3 4

Plan: Organize Ideas

Claim	Reasons
It is important to treat archaeological sites with respect because . . .	One reason to treat achaeological sites with respect is . . .

Relevant Evidence

Source 1	Source 2	Source 3

Draft: Sentence Structure

Sentence Variety Strong writers use different strategies to improve their sentence structure so that their ideas are clear and easy to follow. Sometimes they write their ideas very concisely, so their sentences are straightforward. Other times, they combine short, choppy sentences to create one smoother sentence.

Here is an example: *Chris knows the neighbor is friendly. He knows the neighbor is kind. He knows the neighbor is helpful.* These short and repetitive sentences all describe things Chris knows about the same neighbor, so they can be combined. *Chris knows the neighbor is friendly, kind, and helpful.* This makes it clear that the writer is talking about the same neighbor.

Read the sentence below. How might you revise it to combine ideas? Do you need to change the order of any ideas?

> There are many ancient Egyptian pyramids. Many are tombs for pharaohs. Many have multiple chambers.

_____

_____

Draft Use your graphic organizer and the information above to write your draft in your writer's notebook. Before you start writing, review the rubric on page 98. Remember to indent each paragraph. Also, remember to use transitional words such as *for example, therefore,* or *finally* to organize and connect ideas more clearly within a sentence or between paragraphs.

Grammar Connections

Remember these proofreading rules:

- Compound subjects and predicates can use **coordinating conjunctions** (*and, or*) or **correlative conjunctions** (*either/or, neither/nor*).

- Use **commas** to separate three or more words or phrases in a series.

- Use commas to set off **introductory words** in sentences.

CHECK IN 1 2 3 4

Revise: Peer Conferences

Review a Draft Listen actively to your partner. Take notes about what you liked and what was difficult to follow. Begin by telling what you liked. Use these sentence starters.

Your conclusion was convincing because . . .
What do you think about rearranging this sentence . . .
I think adding more examples of strong language can help to . . .

After you finish giving each other feedback, reflect on the peer conference. What suggestion did you find to be the most helpful?

_____

_____

_____

Revising Checklist

☑ Revising Checklist

☐ Do my ideas makes sense? Are they clear and easy to follow?

☐ Did I include enough relevant evidence to support my argument?

☐ Did I vary my sentence structure by combining or rearranging ideas?

☐ Did I use examples of strong language in my conclusion?

☐ Did I check my spelling and punctuation?

Revision Use the Revising Checklist to help you figure out what text you may need to move, elaborate on, or delete. After you finish writing your final draft, use the full rubric on pages 236–239 to score your essay.

Turn to page 85. Fill in the bars to show what you learned.

My Score			
Purpose, Focus, & Organization (4 pts)	Evidence & Elaboration (4 pts)	Conventions (2 pts)	Total (10 pts)

My Goal I can read and understand social studies texts.

TAKE NOTES

Take notes and annotate as you read the passages "Teamwork and Destiny" and "US Space School."

Look for the answer to the question: *Why is it important for people to work in teams to solve problems?*

_____

_____

_____

_____

_____

_____

_____

_____

_____

_____

_____

PASSAGE 1

NARRATIVE NONFICTION

Teamwork and DESTINY

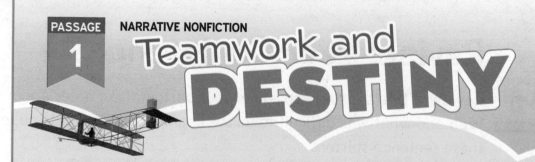

The wind was strong on December 17, 1903, near Kitty Hawk, North Carolina. That day, Wilbur and Orville Wright's perseverance paid off. From a hill near the Atlantic Ocean, the brothers launched an aircraft using a gasoline-powered engine. The flight lasted only twelve seconds, but it guaranteed the Wright brothers a place in history.

Wilbur was born on April 16, 1867, and Orville, on August 19, 1871, in Ohio. From an early age, both boys showed strong mechanical abilities. In 1878, their father gave them a toy helicopter powered by a rubber band. The brothers built their own copies, and their lifelong interest in flying began.

The Wrights' first business was a printing shop. Next, they opened a bicycle shop and began manufacturing their own bicycles. The wheels of history then turned toward their destiny as they began experimenting with kites, hoping to build a flying machine.

The brothers' experiments led them to Kitty Hawk, where wind was nearly constant. In 1900, they built their first glider capable of holding a pilot, which flew for ten seconds. The next year, they constructed a larger model. The 1901 model did not have enough lift, or an uplifting force created as wings move though air. But the brothers did not give up. They then built a wind tunnel to help test their models. In 1902, they produced a third glider, which became fully controllable after hundreds of tests.

Library of Congress Prints and Photographs Division [LC-DIG-ppprs-00699]

The next step was especially challenging—creating an engine-powered aircraft. The Wrights enlisted the help of their mechanic, Charles Taylor. He helped them design a lightweight gasoline engine powerful enough to propel aircraft. By 1905, the team created a practical plane, able to remain in the air until its fuel ran out. The Wrights' determination and teamwork led to one of the greatest inventions of the twentieth century.

PASSAGE 2

EXPOSITORY TEXT

US Space SCHOOL

NASA is the US government agency that has overseen Apollo and other space programs. Ongoing projects include making a satellite to measure changes in the oceans. Most NASA workers have interests in science and engineering. Yet the agency also has to run like a business. For example, NASA has to acquire materials and follow schedules. In the 1990s, officials realized the agency needed development in this and other ways. So NASA built a school to better organize its teams and their work.

Team Players

Richard Lynch has managed the teams building the Webb Telescope. "It's my job to make sure that all the different parts of the spacecraft are built properly," he explains. The telescope needs many functions, such as controls for overheating and for communication. "We have different teams for each of these elements," he says. Managers like Lynch have proven leadership skills, but they also get training to keep improving teamwork. According to Lynch, "Teamwork and collaboration

TAKE NOTES

TAKE NOTES

are critical." He meets with each team every week to talk about any issues. Every week, they share updates about problems and discuss possible solutions. Lynch delegates, or assigns, projects to other team members as needed so that everyone has a role in the team's success.

People Skills

NASA offers one class called Quiet Project Management. This class helps workers respect one another. It also helps workers recognize the positive qualities in team members and play to their strengths. With its classes and training, NASA recognizes the importance of lifelong learning—not just in technology, but in organizing and team building.

This photograph shows James Irwin, a NASA astronaut on the *Apollo 15* flight. He is shown saluting on the moon on August 1971.

COMPARE THE PASSAGES

Review your notes from "Teamwork and Destiny" and "US Space School."
Use your notes and the Venn diagram below to record how the information
in the passages is alike and different.

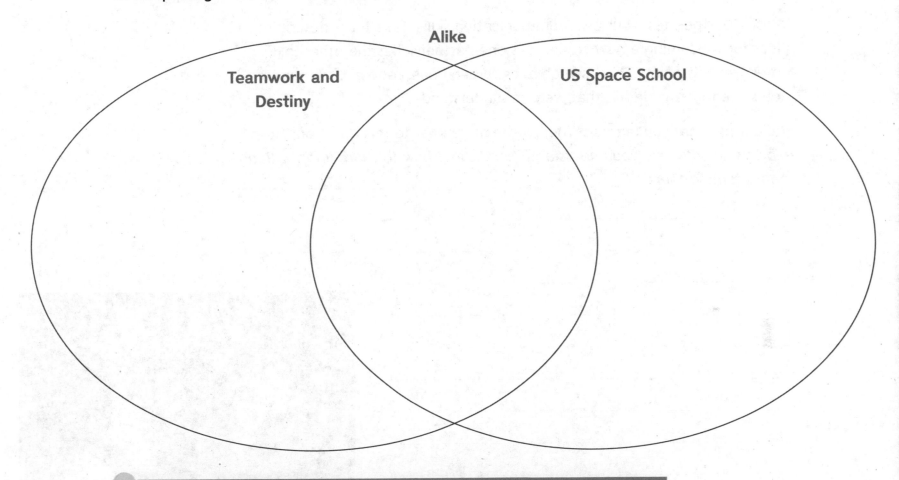

Alike

Teamwork and Destiny

US Space School

Synthesize Information

Think about what you learned from both texts. Why is teamwork so
important to successful air and space exploration? Write your ideas in
your reader's notebook.

CHECK IN 1 2 3 4

SHARE AND REFLECT

COLLABORATE

Good communication helps teams work together effectively. To communicate well, both sender and receiver must understand the information being passed.

With a partner, test your own communication skills. Take turns describing ideas for welcoming a new student. As one partner talks, the other takes notes while listening. Then, switch roles. When done, read each other's notes. Identify any details that were misunderstood.

Reflect on what you learned. Then, write an answer to this question: *How did this activity help you understand more about how to share information and listen to others?* _____

_____

_____

_____

_____

_____

_____

_____

kali9/iStock/Getty Images

MAKE A TEAMWORK POSTER

Use your background knowledge and the texts you have read in this unit. With a partner, brainstorm ways people work together, either one-on-one or as a team. As you take turns sharing ideas, write your ideas down.

_____

_____

_____

With your partner, create a poster about a local team. It can be a real team in your community or one that the two of you made up. The team you choose should raise awareness about a community concern. Your poster must include a picture and some words that describe the team and how it helps the community. Use the ideas you brainstormed if you need help.

_____

_____

_____

Share your poster with a small group. Be sure to explain why you think it is important to work together. What have you learned after watching the other presentations? Answer in three sentences. _____

_____

_____

TAKE NOTES

Take notes and annotate as you read the passages "To Be an Archaeologist" and "Digging Into the Past."

Look for the answer to these questions: *Why is planning an important part of archaeology? How does planning help with researching, studying, and preserving past civilizations?*

_____

_____

_____

_____

_____

_____

_____

PASSAGE 1 EXPOSITORY TEXT

To Be an Archaeologist

What is the oldest thing you own? Some people keep old photos and books. Other people hand down special items from grandparents to parents to children. For example, you may know someone who has something a grandparent made by hand.

The past is interesting to most people. But archaeologists are so interested in exploring the past that they make it their job to study how people lived long ago. They dig in areas of ancient settlements to examine the remains, and they study and report on ancient culture. Does this sound like something you might like to do as a career?

Duties

Archaeologists use their knowledge of the sciences and social studies to plan research projects. They determine how people lived in the past and report their findings, so the information can be used to piece together a history of people. Archaeologists study findings in many kinds of places, including construction and underwater sites.

Archaeologists use measuring tools, laboratory and recording equipment, and related software, such as technology that tracks locations. Many people with advanced degrees in archaeology teach at schools or work at museums. Some work for the government. Archaeologists often work in rugged and remote sites around the world.

Education

Those who do fieldwork must usually have a bachelor's degree. Working in positions of authority usually requires more advanced degrees. The skills needed include the abilities to make observations, think critically, analyze data, draw conclusions, and communicate findings.

PASSAGE 2   **INTERVIEW**

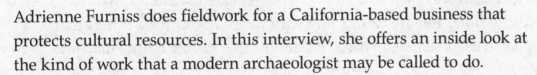

Adrienne Furniss does fieldwork for a California-based business that protects cultural resources. In this interview, she offers an inside look at the kind of work that a modern archaeologist may be called to do.

Q: What kind of work is involved?

A: Groups like ours get called in when something new is being built or when people are doing maintenance on electrical lines, plumbing, or similar underground features. We get called in to make sure that nothing of importance is being destroyed without being recorded or preserved.

Q: Like what?

A: The things we look for include human burial grounds and settlements. For example, we recently uncovered the foundations of an old tannery underneath some university buildings. We found old rusted equipment, wooden and concrete beams, old glass bottles, and even leather hides that could be one hundred years old or older.

TAKE NOTES

Danny Daniels/Stockbyte/Getty Images

TAKE NOTES

_____

_____

_____

_____

_____

_____

_____

_____

_____

_____

_____

_____

_____

_____

_____

_____

Q: What are the challenges?

A: The work is very hard physically. You have to be able to carry buckets of soil that can weigh up to 60 pounds. You help move large amounts of equipment. We use all kinds of digging tools to remove soil from sites, so our arms can get tired.

We also have to use our minds. For example, we study the smallest differences in soil color and composition. These differences can be clues that something was once there, and the clues can help us plan the best steps to take.

Q: What do you like about the work?

A: History stops being abstract. It's not just read about in a book.

I love using my own two hands to help make discoveries that have been lost to time. You are connecting with the past, touching things that people used on a daily basis. It's almost like having a time machine.

COMPARE THE PASSAGES

Review your notes from "To Be an Archaeologist" and "Digging Into the Past." Use your notes and the Venn diagram below to record how the information in the passages is alike and different.

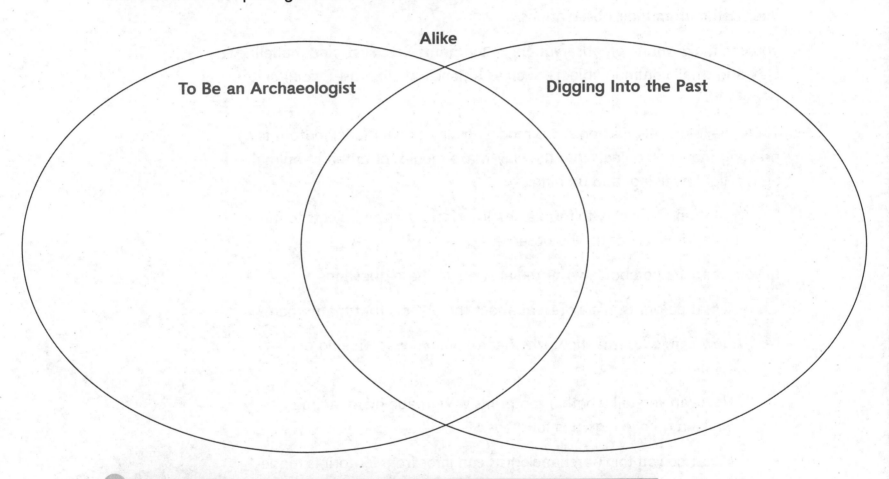

Alike

To Be an Archaeologist

Digging Into the Past

Synthesize Information

Think about both texts and the texts you read in this unit. How does studying our past help us understand how people once lived? Write your answer in your reader's notebook.

CHECK IN ⟩ 1 ⟩ 2 ⟩ 3 ⟩ 4 ⟩

CONNECT TO CONTENT

MAKE OBSERVATIONS OF FOOTPRINTS

Archaeologists use evidence to find out about life in the past. Evidence can be anything old, from fossils to even footprints left behind on rocks. They make observations about the evidence they find, and they interpret the information from their observations.

You can make your own observations of footprints, too. First, find modeling clay and small common objects, such as a pencil, shell, eraser, coin, or paper clip.

Then, make models. Flatten some modeling clay. Make model footprints by pressing the small objects into the clay. Make models of different animals—heavy, light, walking, and running.

Finally, flatten some clay to form a small surface. Use the objects to make model footprints. What do you observe?

In your reader's notebook, write the answers to these questions:

- What do prints in clay reveal about the objects that made them?

- How can footprints show whether an animal was walking or running?

- How can you tell whether footprints were made by an animal walking on two legs? On four legs?

- What do you think archaeologists can infer from footprints made long ago?

Reflect on Your Learning

Talk About It Reflect on what you learned in this unit. Then talk with a partner about how you did.

I am really proud of how I can _____

_____

_____

_____

Something I need to work more on is _____

_____

_____

_____

My Goal Set a goal for Unit 4. In your reader's notebook, write about what you can do to get there.

Share a goal you have with a partner.

? Essential Question

What can people do to bring about a positive change?

Build Vocabulary

Write new words you learned about how people can challenge unfair laws. Draw lines and circles for the words you write.

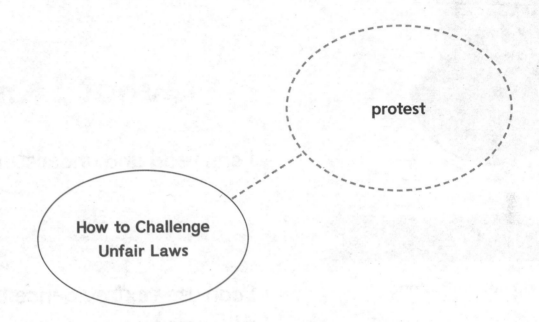

protest

How to Challenge
Unfair Laws

Go online to **my.mheducation.com** and read the "Liberty and Justice for All" Blast. Think about the freedoms and rights that we have today in the United States. What would you do if you did not have those rights? Then blast back your response.

MY GOALS

Think about what you already know. Fill in the bars. This will be a good start.

Key

1 =	I do not understand.
2 =	I understand but need more practice.
3 =	I understand.
4 =	I understand and can teach someone.

What I Know Now

I can read and understand a biography.

I can use text evidence to respond to a biography.

I know there are ways people can bring about a positive change.

1 2 3 4

 You will come back to the next page later.

Think about what you learned. Fill in the bars. What are you getting better at?

What I Learned

I can read and understand a biography.

1 2 3 4

I can use text evidence to respond to a biography.

1 2 3 4

I know there are ways people can bring about a positive change.

1 2 3 4

My Goal I can read and understand a biography.

TAKE NOTES

As you read, make note of interesting words and important information.

_____
_____
_____
_____
_____
_____
_____
_____
_____
_____
_____
_____
_____
_____
_____

FREDERICK DOUGLASS

Freedom's Voice

Essential Question

What can people do to bring about a positive change?

Read about what Frederick Douglass did to bring about positive change for African Americans.

Growing Up With Slavery

When Frederick Douglass was growing up in Maryland, he never could have imagined that he would become a great civil rights leader. Born Frederick Bailey, he was enslaved, or living in slavery, until the age of twenty. Frederick's life was difficult. He never knew his father and was separated from his mother at a young age. If he dared to **defy** his "master" in any way, he was punished. One of the few bright spots of his youth was being taught to read by the wife of a slaveholder. Perhaps it was his love of words, along with his courage, that inspired Frederick to reach for the kind of life he was **entitled** to have.

▼ This etching depicts a slave auction, a common event of the time.

A Life-Changing Speech

In 1838, Frederick **sought** his freedom by escaping to the North. In New York City, he married Anna Murray. Then he and Anna moved to New Bedford, Massachusetts.

In New Bedford, Frederick changed his last name to Douglass to protect himself against slave catchers. That was just the first of many changes. He also discovered a group of people—abolitionists—who shared his hope of ending slavery. He had read about the abolition movement in William Lloyd Garrison's newspaper, *The Liberator*. Frederick devoured every issue because the ideas inspired him so much. Soon he began speaking against slavery at the church meetings he attended.

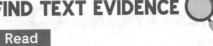

FIND TEXT EVIDENCE 🔍

Read

Paragraph 1

Author's Perspective

Underline two details that tell about slavery. What is the author's perspective?

_____

_____

Paragraphs 2–3

Summarize

Summarize Douglass's life in the North.

_____

_____

_____

_____

_____

Reread

Author's Craft

Why does the author provide background on Douglass's early life?

FIND TEXT EVIDENCE

Read

Paragraphs 1–3

Summarize

Summarize Douglass's feelings before, during, and after speaking at the Anti-Slavery Society.

_____

_____

_____

_____

_____

Paragraph 4

Author's Perspective

Circle the words that show how the author feels about Douglass as a speaker.

Reread

Author's Craft

Why is the audience's response to Douglass's speech significant?

New Opportunities

In 1841, the Massachusetts Anti-Slavery Society held a meeting in Nantucket. Frederick was eager to hear the abolitionist speakers and traveled to the meeting with **anticipation**. However, when he arrived, something totally unexpected happened. An abolitionist who had heard Frederick speak at a church meeting asked him to speak to this large gathering!

Frederick went to the front of the meeting hall, trembling with fright. At first, he spoke quietly and hesitantly. He felt anxious standing in front of so many people—especially white people! However, once he got started, his fear evaporated. He spoke from his heart, describing the horrors of slavery. Frederick was a stirring speaker, articulate and **outspoken**. At the end of his speech, the audience's reaction was spontaneous—suddenly everyone stood up and cheered! Among those cheering was none other than William Lloyd Garrison.

After the meeting, Garrison congratulated Frederick and offered him a job as a speaker for the society. Frederick agreed and was hired as a full-time lecturer. He felt he had found a purpose for his life.

Frederick traveled through New England and the Midwest, giving passionate speeches that captivated audiences. It was impossible to listen to his powerful words and remain **neutral**. Frederick had a commanding presence and spoke with eloquence and dignity. He was making a name for himself.

North Wind Picture Archives/Alamy Stock Photo

Making His Mark

In addition to giving speeches, Frederick had time **reserved** for his writing. In 1845 he wrote an autobiography, *Narrative of the Life of Frederick Douglass, an American Slave*. The book became a huge success, making him even more famous.

In his autobiography, Frederick revealed that he was a fugitive. For his safety, friends suggested that he go on a speaking tour in Great Britain. Frederick was very popular there, and people lined up to hear him speak.

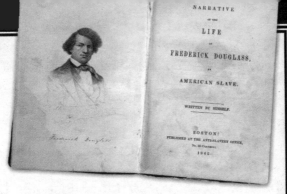

▲ Douglass's autobiography helped advance abolition.

In 1847, Frederick returned to the United States. By now, he had a family and missed them terribly. Upon his return, they moved to Rochester, New York, where Frederick started his own abolitionist newspaper. *The North Star* was an unusual newspaper. It published articles not only about the antislavery cause, but also about the **unequal** status of women. Frederick also worked tirelessly to end segregation in Rochester's schools.

▲ *The North Star* was the newspaper published by Frederick Douglass and his wife.

Summarize

Use your notes and the illustrations, photos, and captions to orally summarize what you learned about Frederick Douglass.

FIND TEXT EVIDENCE 🔍

Read

Paragraph 1
Suffixes

The suffix *-ive* means "having the nature of." How does the suffix help you determine the meaning of *narrative*? Write your answer here.

_____

_____

_____

Paragraphs 2–3
Photographs and Captions

What do the photographs show?

_____

_____

Underline the new information about Douglass in the captions.

Reread
Author's Craft

Why do you think the author used the subhead "Making His Mark" for this section of the text?

Vocabulary

Use the example sentences to talk with a partner about each word. Then answer the questions.

anticipation

The goalie waited with **anticipation** as the ball came toward her.

What is something that you have waited for with anticipation?

My birthday.

defy

If you **defy** a driving rule, you may get a ticket.

Why might someone defy a rule or law?

If it's unfair or if there is an emergency

entitled

The library card **entitled** Matt to check out a book.

What phrase has the same meaning as *entitled*?

allowed a

neutral

An umpire must stay **neutral** when making a call on a play.

Why must an umpire or referee stay neutral during a game?

So they are not biased.

outspoken

Jake is **outspoken** about protecting the environment.

What word has the opposite meaning of *outspoken*?

Soft spoken

Build Your Word List Pick a word you found interesting in the selection you read. Look up synonyms and antonyms of the word in a thesaurus, and write them in your reader's notebook. Check your work for accuracy in a reference source.

reserved

Some parking spaces are **reserved** for people with babies.

What other things can be reserved?

dinner tables and seats to a game or concert

sought

Josie **sought** the missing puzzle piece.

What was something you sought and were able to find?

_____

_____

_____

unequal

The number of players on the tug-of-war teams was **unequal**.

If two teams are unequal, what might the game be like?

one team will have an advantage

_____

Prefixes and Suffixes

Prefixes are added to the beginnings of words and change their meanings. The prefix *un-* means "not." The prefix *en-* means "to make." **Suffixes** are added to the ends of words and change their meanings. The suffix *–ive* means "having the nature of." The suffixes *–er* and *–or* mean "a person who."

🔍 FIND TEXT EVIDENCE

When I read the word enslaved, *I can use the prefix* en- *to figure out the meaning of the word. Since* en- *means "to make,"* enslaved *must mean "made a slave."*

Born Frederick Bailey, he was enslaved, or living in slavery, until the age of twenty.

Your Turn Use the prefix or suffix to figure out the meanings of the following words in "Frederick Douglass: Freedom's Voice."

liberator, *page 127* _____

unexpected, *page 128* _____

CHECK IN ▷ 1 ▷ 2 ▷ 3 ▷ 4

Todd Bigelow/Aurora Photos

Summarize

When you summarize, you sort the central idea and relevant details and use your own words to state them. This helps you to monitor comprehension and remember what you have learned. Reread, use background knowledge, and ask questions to make adjustments as you read.

FIND TEXT EVIDENCE

To make sure you understand the most relevant details of "Growing Up With Slavery" on page 127, you summarize the most important points.

> **Page 127**
>
> Born Frederick Bailey, he was enslaved, or living in slavery, until the age of twenty. Frederick's life was difficult. He never knew his father and was separated from his mother at a young age. If he dared to **defy** his "master" in any way, he was punished. One of the few bright spots of his youth was being taught to read by the wife of a slaveholder. Perhaps it was his love of words, along with his courage, that inspired Frederick to reach for the kind of life he was **entitled** to have.

Frederick Douglass spent the first twenty years of his life in slavery. He was sent away from his mother at an early age, was punished by his "master," and was taught to read by a slaveholder's wife. Learning to read inspired him.

Your Turn Use the central idea and relevant details to summarize the rest of the biography. Use the Summarize strategy as you read other texts.

_____

_____

_____

_____

CHECK IN   1 〉 2 〉 3 〉 4 〉

Photographs and Captions

The selection "Frederick Douglass: Freedom's Voice" is a biography. A biography tells facts about the life of a real person. It describes the person's talents and achievements. A biography is often written in logical order and often includes text features such as **photographs** and **captions**.

🔍 FIND TEXT EVIDENCE

I can tell that "Frederick Douglass: Freedom's Voice" is a biography. Frederick Douglass was a real person. The photographs show real pages from his autobiography and newspaper. The captions give details about the photos. His life events, including his achievements, are told in logical order.

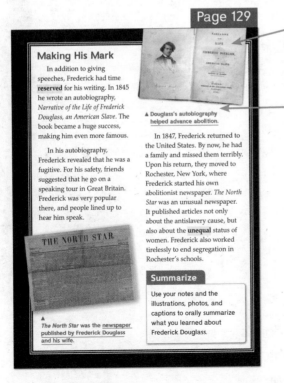

Page 129

Making His Mark

In addition to giving speeches, Frederick had time **reserved** for his writing. In 1845 he wrote an autobiography, *Narrative of the Life of Frederick Douglass, an American Slave*. The book became a huge success, making him even more famous.

In his autobiography, Frederick revealed that he was a fugitive. For his safety, friends suggested that he go on a speaking tour in Great Britain. Frederick was very popular there, and people lined up to hear him speak.

▲ Douglass's autobiography helped advance abolition.

In 1847, Frederick returned to the United States. By now, he had a family and missed them terribly. Upon his return, they moved to Rochester, New York, where Frederick started his own abolitionist newspaper. *The North Star* was an unusual newspaper. It published articles not only about the antislavery cause, but also about the **unequal** status of women. Frederick also worked tirelessly to end segregation in Rochester's schools.

THE NORTH STAR

▲ *The North Star* was the <u>newspaper</u> published by Frederick Douglass and his wife.

Summarize

Use your notes and the illustrations, photos, and captions to orally summarize what you learned about Frederick Douglass.

Photographs

Photographs help readers better visualize the world of the subject of a biography.

Captions

Captions provide additional information.

Your Turn List three examples that show that "Frederick Douglass: Freedom's Voice" is a biography.

_____

_____

_____

_____

CHECK IN ⟩ 1 ⟩ 2 ⟩ 3 ⟩ 4

Author's Perspective

An **author's perspective** is the author's attitude toward the person or subject he or she is writing about. You can determine an author's perspective by looking at the details, descriptions, and the reasons and evidence for points the author makes.

🔍 FIND TEXT EVIDENCE

On page 127, the words tell that the author thinks highly of Frederick Douglass. The author says that Douglass would become a great civil rights leader.

Details	Author's Perspective
He would become a great civil rights leader.	Frederick was an extraordinary person because he became a great civil rights leader in spite of his difficult beginning in life.
Frederick had a difficult life in slavery.	
Love of words and his own courage inspired him.	

Your Turn Reread the rest of "Frederick Douglass: Freedom's Voice." Record details about Frederick's life in the graphic organizer on page 135. Then tell the author's perspective.

CHECK IN 1 > 2 > 3 > 4

Details	Author's Perspective

Respond to Reading

COLLABORATE

Discuss the prompt below. Use your notes and text evidence to support your answer.

Explain the significance of Frederick Douglass's relationship with the abolitionists.

_____

_____

_____

_____

_____

_____

_____

_____

_____

_____

_____

_____

_____

_____

_____

_____

Quick Tip

Use these sentence starters to discuss the text.

- _When he was young, Frederick Douglass was . . ._

- _After he escaped from slavery, Douglass . . ._

- _The abolitionists helped Douglass by . . ._

Grammar Connections

As you write, check that any pronouns you use have a clear antecedent. For example: Garrison congratulated Frederick and offered **him** a job.

The pronoun _him_ refers back to Frederick and not to Garrison.

CHECK IN 1 2 3 4

Positive Change

COLLABORATE

Many people brought about positive changes for civil rights. Research one person who was involved with the civil rights movement. Then design a plaque in honor of that person. Include a brief history of the person. Work collaboratively with a partner.

Tech Tip

You can type your bibliography on a computer. Here is an example entry for a book about civil rights: Smith, Joan. *Civil Rights*. New York: Example Publishers, 2018.

Step 1 **Set a Goal** Think about the person you chose. Why was this person an important part of the civil rights movement?

Step 2 **Identify Sources** Discuss the print sources or websites you will use to research information.

Step 3 **Find and Record Information** Take notes and cite your sources.

Why is it important to cite your sources?

_____

_____

Step 4 **Organize and Synthesize Information** Draft your plaque. Discuss any art you may want to include. Use your notes to write a brief history of the person. Then develop a bibliography of all the sources you used. A bibliography is a list of the print and online sources you used to research your topic. If you need help creating the entries of your bibliography, ask your teacher or another adult. Each source will be its own entry.

Step 5 **Create and Present** Design a final version of your plaque. Think about adding a quote from the person or a quote about the person to your plaque. After you finish, present your work to the class.

Dr. Martin Luther King, Jr. (1929–1968) was a civil rights leader whose actions led to positive changes.

CHECK IN ⟩ 1 ⟩ 2 ⟩ 3 ⟩ 4 ⟩

Consolidated News Pictures/Contributor/Hulton Archive

Rosa

 How does the author help you visualize what Rosa was like?

Literature Anthology:
pages 262–277

COLLABORATE

Talk About It Reread the last paragraph on **Literature Anthology** page 265. Discuss with your partner what Rosa does when she sits on the bus.

Cite Text Evidence What words and phrases help create a mental image of what Rosa was like? Write text evidence in the chart.

 Evaluate Information

Illustrations can help you to understand the text. How does the illustration help you to visualize Rosa and understand what kind of person she was?

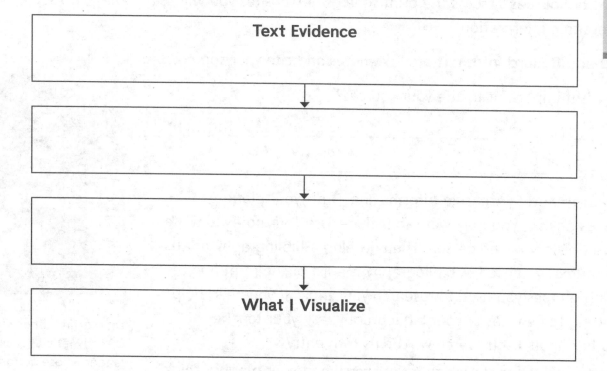

Text Evidence

↓

↓

↓

What I Visualize

Write The author helps me understand what Rosa was like by _____

_____

CHECK IN 1 2 3 4

? **How do you know what Rosa thinks and how she feels as she sits on the bus waiting for the police?**

Talk About It Reread **Literature Anthology** page 268. Turn to a partner, and talk about what Rosa thinks about on the bus.

Cite Text Evidence What words and phrases help you know what Rosa is thinking and feeling? Write text evidence in the chart.

What Rosa Thinks	What It Shows

Write I know what Rosa is thinking and feeling on the bus because

the author _____

_____

_____

CHECK IN 1 2 3 4

? **Why does the author use Martin Luther King, Jr.'s quote?**

COLLABORATE

Talk About It Reread the last paragraph on **Literature Anthology** page 272. Turn to a partner and talk about what Martin Luther King, Jr. said.

Cite Text Evidence What does Martin Luther King, Jr.'s quote mean? Cite text evidence, and tell why the author includes it in the selection.

Quick Tip

Figurative language such as similes and metaphors contributes to the author's overall message. A simile compares two things using *like* or *as*. A metaphor compares two things without using *like* or *as*. As you read, look for *like* or *as* and think about what is being compared.

Text Evidence	→	What It Means
	→	
	→	

Write The author uses Martin Luther King, Jr.'s quote to help me

understand _____

_____

CHECK IN 1 2 3 4

Ian Dagnall Commercial Collection/Alamy Stock Photo

Respond to Reading

Discuss the prompt below. Use your notes and text evidence to support your response.

Describe three lessons from Rosa Parks's actions and explain them using text evidence.

_____

_____

_____

_____

_____

_____

_____

_____

_____

_____

_____

CHECK IN 1 2 3 4

Our Voices, Our Votes

Literature Anthology:
pages 280–283

Rights for African Americans

1   During the early 1800s, many women's groups joined with abolitionists to demand equal rights. Abolitionists were people who wanted to end slavery. They believed that freedom was a natural right. Women marched with them in protest. Some of them helped enslaved people escape to places where they could be free. Over 300 people gathered at a convention in Seneca Falls, New York, in 1848. They discussed how women's rights were linked to other social and civil rights movements. Some speakers urged that suffrage, or voting rights, be a top priority for African Americans and women.

2   After the Civil War, the United States government added the Thirteenth Amendment, outlawing slavery. Three years later, the Fourteenth Amendment granted former slaves rights as citizens. Finally, in 1870, the Fifteenth Amendment gave male citizens of all races the right to vote. Though many women supported these causes, women still could not vote. Their fight was far from over.

Reread paragraph 1. **Circle** the sentence that helps you understand who abolitionists were.

Then **underline** the sentence that explains how the abolitionists and women who wanted suffrage were alike.

COLLABORATE

Reread paragraph 2. Talk with a partner about how the author organizes information. **Write** numbers in the margin to indicate the order in which the laws changed.

Women's Suffrage

[3]   Women continued to fight for suffrage on the national, state, and local levels. Some were outraged enough to defy voting laws and attempt to cast ballots in elections. These acts of civil disobedience resulted in fines. In some cases, the women ended up in jail.

[4]   Women's suffrage remained unpopular with many men. Even so, the idea took hold in some areas. In 1869, Wyoming became the first state to allow women to vote in its elections. Over the next twenty years, four more states would grant women this right.

[5]   Women began to join forces, borrowing ideas from women's groups in other countries. Some hired lobbyists, or people who tried to convince politicians to vote a certain way. Others held huge rallies to raise awareness. Petitions bearing thousands of signatures demanded that the country's laws be amended.

[6]   President Woodrow Wilson finally agreed that a true democracy should not deny women the right to vote. With his support, Congress drafted the Nineteenth Amendment to the Constitution. In 1920, it was approved.

How do you know that suffrage was an important issue for women? **Underline** the clue in paragraph 3 that helps you understand how big a struggle it was.

Reread paragraph 5. **Circle** the ways women took action. Write them here:

1. _____

2. _____

3. _____

4. _____

Talk with a partner about how President Woodrow Wilson influenced how women achieved the right to vote. **Draw a box** around the text evidence to support your discussion.

Why is "Our Voices, Our Votes" a good title for this selection?

COLLABORATE

Talk About It Reread paragraph 5 on page 143. Talk with a partner about how women joined forces to make changes in the law.

Cite Text Evidence What words and phrases help you understand how women worked together to change the voting laws? Write text evidence.

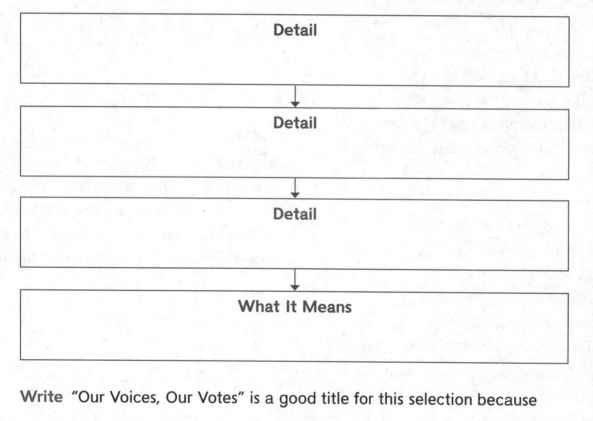

Detail

↓

Detail

↓

Detail

↓

What It Means

Write "Our Voices, Our Votes" is a good title for this selection because

_____

_____

_____

Evaluate Information

A voice is made up of sounds, but a voice is also an opinion or choice. Why do you think the author uses the word *voices* in the title?

Abigail Adams supported women's right to vote.

CHECK IN ⟩ 1 ⟩ 2 ⟩ 3 ⟩ 4 ⟩

Chronology

As authors plan their writing, they think about how to best structure their text in a logical order so that it contributes to their purpose. For example, authors who write informational text about historical events may structure text in chronological order, or the order in which events happen in time.

 FIND TEXT EVIDENCE

On page 142 of "Our Voices, Our Votes," the author structures paragraph 2 in a logical time order to show when constitutional amendments granted rights to males but not women.

> Finally, in 1870, the Fifteenth Amendment gave male citizens of all races the right to vote.

 Your Turn Reread paragraph 4 under "Women's Suffrage" on page 143.

- Why does the author tell about what happened in Wyoming at this point in the text?

_____

_____

- How does this contribute to the author's purpose?

_____

_____

_____

Readers to Writers

Before you begin writing, plan a logical order of what you want to say. For historical events, it makes sense to structure your text in time order. Within that structure, think about what is most important to include.

CHECK IN 1 2 3 4

? How does the information in the photograph, *Rosa,* and "Our Voices, Our Votes" help you understand how people can take a stand?

COLLABORATE

Talk About It Look at the photograph. Read the caption. Talk with a partner about the signs the students are holding.

Cite Text Evidence In the photograph, **circle** what the students support. In the caption, **underline** what they are taking a stand against.

Write The information in the photograph, *Rosa,* and "Our Voices, Our Votes" shows how people take a stand by _____

_____

_____

_____

_____

_____

_____

_____

Rawpixel/iStock/Getty Images

> **Quick Tip**
>
> Look closely at the students in the photograph. What do their expressions and body language show how they feel about what they are supporting?

Be Kind!

STAND UP AGAINST BULLYING!

A group of students supports an anti-bullying movement.

CHECK IN ▶ 1 ▷ 2 ▷ 3 ▷ 4 ▷

My Goal I know there are ways people can bring about a positive change.

Create a Podcast

How did the people you learned about effect positive changes for civil and equal rights? Write an introduction for a podcast featuring these people. Use text evidence to support your ideas.

1. Look at your Build Knowledge notes in your reader's notebook.

2. Think about what qualities the people you read about have in common. Use your ideas to write an introduction for a podcast. Be sure to use examples from the texts you read.

3. Make sure to write about what effect these people had on civil and equal rights. Use new vocabulary words.

Think about what you learned in this text set. Fill in the bars on page 125.

Build Knowledge

Build Vocabulary

Write new words you learned about what discoveries you can make when you give things a second look. Draw lines and circles for the words you write.

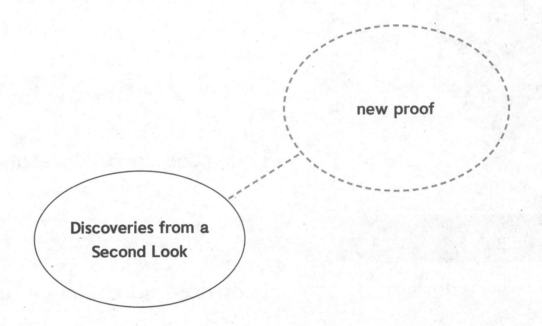

new proof

Discoveries from a Second Look

Go online to **my.mheducation.com** and read the "A Second Glance" Blast. Do you know of any mysteries? What have you discovered when you gave things a second look? Blast back your response.

Unit 4 • Text Set 2   149

Think about what you already know. Fill in the bars. It's okay if you want more practice.

What I Know Now

Key
1 = I do not understand.
2 = I understand but need more practice.
3 = I understand.
4 = I understand and can teach someone.

I can read and understand a drama.

1 > 2 > 3 > 4

I can use text evidence to respond to a drama.

1 > 2 > 3 > 4

I know what we can discover when we give things a second look.

1 > 2 > 3 > 4

STOP You will come back to the next page later.

Think about what you learned. Fill in the bars. What progress did you make?

What I Learned

I can read and understand a drama.

1 2 3 4

I can use text evidence to respond to a drama.

1 2 3 4

I know what we can discover when we give things a second look.

1 2 3 4

My Goal
I can read and understand a drama.

TAKE NOTES

As you read, make note of interesting words and important events.

_____

_____

_____

_____

_____

_____

_____

_____

_____

_____

_____

_____

_____

Where's Brownie?

CAST

SAM *and* **ALEX JENSEN:** Twin sisters with different personalities. SAM is athletic and outgoing. ALEX is quiet and studious.

NARRATOR: One of the sisters, ten years later

EVAN: A classmate

NICK: The building superintendent

NICKY: Nick's young son

Elizabeth Buttler

Essential Question

? **What can you discover when you give things a second look?**

Read about kids who piece together clues to find a missing pet.

Scene One

Setting: A two-person bedroom in an apartment. SAM sits at a messy desk, creating a poster. EVAN works at a clean desk. Nearby are an empty terrarium and a paper bag that is wet and torn at the bottom.

Narrator: Whoever claimed that "two heads are better than one" never met my twin sister. Half the time, she makes problems worse rather than better. Like when we lost Brownie, our pet chameleon . . .

(ALEX enters. SAM and EVAN quickly cover up their work.)

Alex: How was the science fair? Did everyone like Brownie?

Sam: They did. Mr. Rollins was **astounded** that my exhibit was so good. *(SAM tries to hide the empty terrarium from ALEX.)*

Alex: So where's Brownie? And why is Evan here?

(EVAN and SAM begin texting on handheld devices.)

Alex: How should I **interpret** this silence? You're making me feel **suspicious**. And where's Brownie?

Sam: Um, Brownie's missing. But look! Evan and I made these.

*(SAM pulls out a poster she had **concealed** on her desk.)*

Sam: We'll put them up at school tomorrow.

Alex: What makes you think Brownie's back at school?

Sam: Because that's the last place I saw him. In that bag.

Alex: Hey, the bottom of the bag is all wet.

Sam: Maybe it got wet in the lobby. Little Nicky was playing in the fountain with his foldy-paper boat thingies.

Alex: That's origami, to be **precise**. Hey! The bag has a rip.

Sam: Rip? I didn't see a rip. Oh, at the bottom.

Alex: Follow me. I think I know where Brownie is!

Narrator: We raced to the lobby. Brownie had been missing for over an hour, but better late than never!

DRAMA

FIND TEXT EVIDENCE

Read

Page 153

Scenes

Circle the information that tells where Scene One takes place.

Stage Directions

Underline what Sam and Evan do when Alex enters. What does this tell you about Sam and Evan?

_____

_____

Narrator's Last Line

Adages and Proverbs

"Better late than never!" is an adage, a traditional saying. Using context, what does it mean?

_____

_____

_____

Reread

Author's Craft

How does the description of the setting create suspense?

FIND TEXT EVIDENCE 🔍

Read

Page 154

Visualize

Use the setting to create mental images of what is happening in the lobby. What do you visualize?

_____

_____

_____

Nick's Dialogue

Character Perspective

Circle the text that tells you what Nick thinks about the kids' problem. What does Nick think the kids should do?

_____

_____

_____

Reread

Author's Craft

Why are the characters able to successfully proceed in their search for Brownie?

Scene Two

Setting: The lobby of the apartment building. A tall, green, potted plant stands next to a small fountain, where NICKY is playing. ALEX, SAM, and EVAN talk to NICK near a bulletin board.

Nick: So these posters are about your lizard, Brownie. I'm still **perplexed** as to why you think he's down here.

Sam: Because we already checked upstairs.

Alex: Brownie's a chameleon. We think he escaped when Sam set the bag down near the fountain.

Nick: Hey, Nicky! Any brown lizards in the lobby?

Nicky: Nope.

Nick: Maybe you should **reconsider** this and try searching your apartment again.

Evan: Wait a minute. *(checks his device)* It says here that chameleons climb trees.

Nick: Nicky! Any brown lizards in that tree?

Nicky: Nope.

Evan: It also says that chameleons prefer running water, like that fountain.

Nick: Nicky! Any brown lizards in the fountain?

Nicky: Nope.

Nick: What else does that thing say?

Sam: Yeah, **inquisitive** minds want to know.

Alex: *(to SAM)* Don't you want to find Brownie, or are you thinking "out of sight, out of mind"?

Sam: He's just a lizard, Alex. I mean chameleon. It's not exactly "absence makes the heart grow fonder."

Evan: Listen to this! Chameleons change color to match their environments when they're confused or afraid.

Alex: Of course! Nicky, any GREEN lizards over there?

Nicky: *(points into the tree)* There's just that one.

Alex: It's Brownie!

Sam: *(confused)* Brownie has always been brown.

Alex: That's because we put only brown things in his cage, like branches and wood chips.

Evan: Maybe you should buy him a green plant.

Sam: And a little fountain.

Nicky: And boats to go sailing!

Narrator: Well, that's how we found our beloved Brownie, and all was well with the world once more!

Summarize

Use your notes to orally summarize the plot of the mystery and how it was solved in "Where's Brownie?" When you summarize, be sure to tell the plot events in logical order.

FIND TEXT EVIDENCE

Read

Page 155

Character Perspective

Underline the text that shows Alex's feelings about Brownie. **Circle** the text that tells Sam's feelings about Brownie. How are Alex's feelings about Brownie different from Sam's?

_____

_____

Visualize

Draw a box around the text that tells what Nicky does. What does this help you visualize?

_____

_____

_____

Reread

Author's Craft

Why does the author include Sam's response, "Inquisitive minds want to know"?

Vocabulary

Use the example sentences to talk with a partner about each word. Then answer the questions.

astounded

Jada was **astounded** by her high score in the video game.

What experiences have astounded you?

_____

_____

concealed

The mask **concealed** the identity of the mysterious superhero.

What other ways have people concealed their identities?

_____

_____

inquisitive

The **inquisitive** girl asked a lot of questions.

How might an inquisitive person find things out?

_____

_____

interpret

My sister is taking a class to learn how to use and **interpret** sign language.

When might you need someone to interpret for you?

_____

_____

perplexed

The complicated math problem **perplexed** Joshua for many hours.

What problems or puzzles have perplexed you the most?

_____

_____

Build Your Word List Reread the "Setting" on page 153. Circle the word _creating_. In your reader's notebook, use a word web to write more forms of the word. For example, write _creative_. Check an online or print dictionary for accuracy. Then identify the meanings of these new words, and use them in sentences.

precise

The nurse made a **precise** measurement of June's height.

What other tasks require someone to be precise?

_____

_____

reconsider

After Cara placed her chess piece, Greta had to **reconsider** her next move.

What is something that might make you reconsider a choice?

_____

_____

suspicious

The dog's owner became **suspicious** when he saw paw prints leading to the chair.

What behavior might make you suspicious of something?

_____

_____

Adages and Proverbs

Adages and proverbs are traditional sayings that are often repeated. You can usually use surrounding words and sentences to help you understand the meaning of an unfamiliar saying.

🔍 FIND TEXT EVIDENCE

On page 153, the narrator of "Where's Brownie?" disagrees with the adage "two heads are better than one." In this case, the "two heads" are her own and her twin's. The saying must mean that two people can solve a problem better than one person. However, since her twin "makes problems worse," the narrator probably prefers to figure out things on her own.

Narrator: Whoever claimed that "two heads are better than one" never met my twin sister.

Your Turn Use context clues to explain the meanings of these adages and proverbs from "Where's Brownie?"

"out of sight, out of mind," page 155 _____

_____

"absence makes the heart grow fonder," page 155

_____

CHECK IN ⟩ 1 ⟩ 2 ⟩ 3 ⟩ 4 ⟩

Visualize

Each scene in a play includes a setting description. The setting tells where the scene takes place. When you read a play, it is helpful to visualize, or picture, the setting of the scene, the characters, and the characters' actions.

 FIND TEXT EVIDENCE

When you read the setting description for Scene One of "Where's Brownie?" on page 153, you may have to slow down and take time to picture what is happening.

> Page 153
>
> Scene One
>
> *Setting: A two-person bedroom in an apartment. SAM sits at a messy desk, creating a poster. EVAN works at a clean desk. Nearby are an empty terrarium and a paper bag that is wet and torn at the bottom.*
>
> **Narrator:** Whoever claimed that "two heads are better than one" never met my twin sister. Half the time, she makes problems worse rather than better. Like when we lost Brownie, our pet chameleon . . .
> *(ALEX enters. SAM and EVAN quickly cover up their work.)*
> **Alex:** How was the science fair? Did everyone like Brownie?

First, I have to picture the room and characters, and I wonder what kind of poster they are making. Also, the sight of an empty terrarium and a wet, torn bag makes me curious as to how all the events are connected.

Quick Tip

The cast list at the beginning of a play can help you visualize the characters. A cast list is part of the play's structure. If you are confused about a character, reread any character description that might be given after a character's name. Take a moment to create mental images of the characters.

 Your Turn Why is it important that Nicky is playing near the fountain in Scene Two? Visualize the events to help you. As you read, remember to use the strategy Visualize.

_____

_____

_____

CHECK IN ⟩ 1 ⟩ 2 ⟩ 3 ⟩ 4 ⟩

Elements of a Play

"Where's Brownie?" is a mystery play, or drama. Plays include dialogue, settings, and stage directions. Plays have one or more acts that can be divided into scenes. Each scene has setting details and stage directions. In each scene, note the characters' dialogue and actions. Knowing how and why the characters respond to events can help you infer their perspectives.

🔍 FIND TEXT EVIDENCE

I can tell that "Where's Brownie?" is a play. It begins with a cast list of the characters' relationships. It is one act divided into two scenes. It has setting details and stage directions. We learn most of the story through dialogue.

Page 154

Scene Two

Setting: The lobby of the apartment building. A tall, green, potted plant stands next to a small fountain, where NICKY is playing. ALEX, SAM, and EVAN talk to NICK near a bulletin board.

Nick: So these posters are about your lizard, Brownie. I'm still **perplexed** as to why you think he's down here.

Sam: Because we already checked upstairs.

Alex: Brownie's a chameleon. We think he escaped when Sam set the bag down near the fountain.

Nick: Hey, Nicky! Any brown lizards in the lobby?

Nicky: Nope.

Nick: Maybe you should **reconsider** this and try searching your apartment again.

Evan: Wait a minute. *(checks his device)* It says here that chameleons climb trees.

Nick: Nicky! Any brown lizards in that tree?

Nicky: Nope.

Evan: It also says that chameleons prefer running water, like that fountain.

Nick: Nicky! Any brown lizards in the fountain?

Nicky: Nope.

Scenes

Plays are often divided into scenes that organize the story.

Stage Directions

Stage directions tell actors how to speak dialogue and where they should move.

COLLABORATE **Your Turn** How do the events in Scene One of "Where's Brownie?" lead to the events in Scene Two? What do you learn from the stage directions in Scene Two?

_____

_____

_____

Readers to Writers

Setting descriptions can also help you understand how the plot moves forward. Writers give specific descriptions of a setting when it is important to the plot. For example, the size and color of the plant is an important element in the plot, so the writer gives details about it. How can setting details advance your plot?

CHECK IN 1 > 2 > 3 > 4

Character Perspective

An author develops a **character's perspective** through dialogue, actions, and behavior. In a play, an author develops a character's perspective mostly through dialogue and occasionally stage directions. Analyzing the characters' dialogue and actions in each scene can also help you determine their relationships and conflicts with other characters.

 FIND TEXT EVIDENCE

On page 153 of "Where's Brownie?" I see the narrator recounting an experience involving her sister and a lost pet. I'll use details in the dialogue to understand how the author develops this character's perspective.

Details	Character's Perspective
Has twin sister who makes "problems worse"	The narrator is one of the sisters. She doesn't get upset at her sister for losing Brownie. Instead, she works with her sister so they can find him. This shows she has a good attitude.
Her pet chameleon named Brownie is lost.	
Worries about finding Brownie in time	

 Your Turn Which sister do you think becomes the narrator ten years after the events of the play? What additional details about this sister's perspective does the author give? Record details in your graphic organizer on page 161.

Quick Tip

In a play, a character who delivers a line of dialogue from his or her first-person point of view is called a **speaker**. But a speaker may be a **narrator**, who gives information from outside of the main action of the play. In this play, the narrator knows firsthand what happened. Which sister is more similar to the narrator? This will help you identify the narrator.

CHECK IN 1 2 3 4

Details	Character's Perspective

Respond to Reading

Discuss the prompt below. Use your notes and text evidence to support your response.

COLLABORATE

Name three character traits that helped the characters solve the mystery and explain how these qualities were useful.

_____

_____

_____

_____

_____

_____

_____

_____

_____

_____

_____

_____

_____

_____

_____

Quick Tip

Use these sentence starters to help you discuss the mystery.

- *At the beginning of the selection, the characters seem . . .*

- *As the mystery unfolds, I learn that . . .*

- *The characters were able to solve the mystery because . . .*

Grammar Connections

As you write, check that the pronouns you use agree with verbs. For example: **They looks** at *the plant in the lobby.* The pronoun *they* is plural, so the verb should be corrected to *look* so that it agrees with the pronoun.

CHECK IN 1 2 3 4

A Second Look

COLLABORATE

Sometimes when you conduct research, you may find information that causes you to rethink what you already know. Conduct research on institutions, such as museums, that offer information about the Underground Railroad. Then draft a letter to one institution requesting more information about the Underground Railroad. Work collaboratively with a partner.

Step 1 **Set a Goal** Generate questions you want to answer with research.

Step 2 **Identify Sources** Discuss how you will gather information from print or online sources.

Step 3 **Find and Record Information** Take notes and cite your sources.

Step 4 **Organize and Synthesize Information** Draft your letter. You are asking for official information, so this is a formal inquiry. You may clarify questions to find the most useful information. For example:
• Does the institution have any special exhibits?
• Does the staff have information they can send you, such as pamphlets, booklets, or a brief history?

If an institution has information about your topic, what is a clarifying question you could ask?

Step 5 **Create and Present** Complete a final version of your letter. After you finish, present your work to the class.

Quick Tip

General Question:

Do you have information about the Underground Railroad?

Clarifying Question:

Do you have primary sources about the Underground Railroad such as letters or diary entries?

✓ Checklist

When you write your letter

☐ Include your return address and the date in the heading.

☐ Make sure the inside address with the person's name and address are correct.

☐ Use formal language in the body of the letter.

☐ Introduce yourself and your reason for writing in the first paragraph.

☐ Make sure your request is clear.

☐ Include a closing signature.

CHECK IN ❯ 1 ❯ 2 ❯ 3 ❯ 4

A Window into History

? **How does the author show that people have different perspectives about turning Grandma J.'s house into a playground?**

Literature Anthology: pages 284–293

Talk About It Reread page 287 in the **Literature Anthology**. Turn to your partner, and discuss how the author shows the different perspectives. Why is Daniel Cruz important to this scene?

Cite Text Evidence What words and phrases tell how each character feels about the house being turned into a playground? Write text evidence in the chart.

Text Evidence	What It Shows

Make Inferences

In plays, the characters' names appear before their dialogue. Look for important words and phrases in the dialogue to infer how each character feels about the playground. What do you think the phrases *not right* and *benefit everyone* reveal about the characters' perspectives?

Write The author shows that people have different perspectives by _____

_____

_____

CHECK IN 1 2 3 4

How does the author build suspense?

COLLABORATE

Talk About It Reread Act 2, Scene 2, on page 290 in the **Literature Anthology**. Turn to your partner, and talk about how the setting details in this scene build suspense.

Cite Text Evidence What details in this scene add to the suspense? Use evidence from the text to support your answers.

Reread Act 2, Scene 2, on page 290

Quick Tip

You can use these sentence starters to talk about how the author builds suspense.

• *The author describes . . .*

• *This makes me want to know . . .*

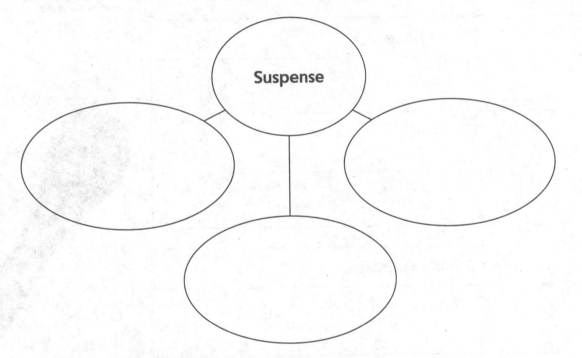

Suspense

Write The author builds suspense in this scene by _____

_____

_____

_____

CHECK IN 1 > 2 > 3 > 4 >

? **Why does the author have Daniel Cruz interview Dr. Cedric Brown about the history of the house?**

Talk About It Reread **Literature Anthology** pages 292 and 293. Turn to your partner, and talk about what Dr. Cedric Brown says.

Cite Text Evidence What words and phrases show that Dr. Cedric Brown's interview is important? Write text evidence in the chart.

Quick Tip

To help come up with answers to fill in the chart, think about the decision to not tear down the house. What did Dr. Cedric Brown say that helped with that decision?

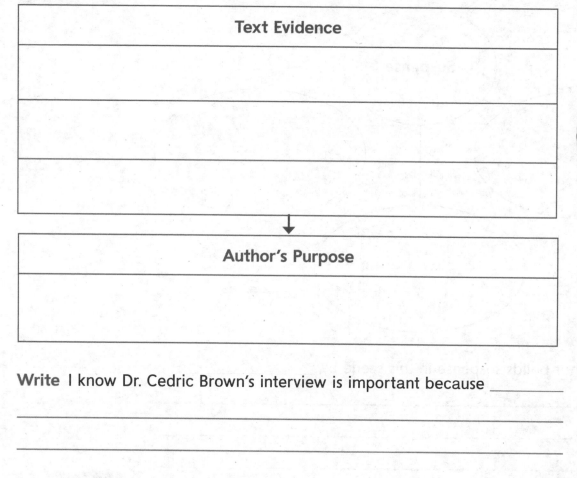

Text Evidence

↓

Author's Purpose

Write I know Dr. Cedric Brown's interview is important because _____

_____

_____

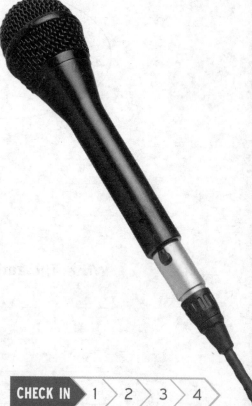

CHECK IN   1   2   3   4

Respond to Reading

COLLABORATE

Discuss the prompt below. Use your notes and text evidence to support your response.

What is the author's purpose for including the two interviews in the play?

_____

_____

_____

_____

_____

_____

_____

_____

_____

_____

_____

_____

_____

Quick Tip

Use these sentence starters to help organize your text evidence.

- *The author uses Daniel Cruz's interviews to . . .*
- *The interviews help the author to . . .*
- *They help me to understand . . .*

CHECK IN 1 2 3 4

A Boy, a Horse, and a Fiddle

Literature Anthology:
pages 296–299

1   Legend tells of a boy who lived with his grandmother in Mongolia a long time ago and cared for her by herding sheep. A tall, well-built youth with a good and honest heart, he loved to sing and play simple homemade instruments.

2   One day, when the boy was out on the steppes, or the grasslands, tending his sheep, he heard a cry—a soft neigh. By a bush, he found a young colt, as white as snow, without its mother. The boy put a rope around its neck and led it home. In the years that followed, he fed and cared for the animal until it grew into a fine stallion that could run like the wind. The boy also grew, and when his work was done, he liked nothing more than to mount his horse and race across the steppes. The horse took much pleasure in listening to the boy sing and play. The two were best friends.

Reread paragraphs 1 and 2. **Underline** the text evidence that describes the setting. Write your answer here:

_____

_____

_____

COLLABORATE

Discuss with a partner the important elements of a legend, such as the historical and cultural setting. Talk about what life would be like living in Mongolia long ago. **Circle** the clues that show what life might have been like. How does the setting influence the plot?

_____

_____

_____

1 The boy was overwhelmed with grief. The following night his horse appeared to him in a dream. Strong and whole, he told the boy:

2 *Make an instrument out of my body. Use my skin to cover the base of the instrument. Use my hair to make two strings, and carve my head out of wood at the top of the fiddle. My ears will guide your sound. I will be with you always as you play and sing, and the music you make will fill people's hearts with joy.*

3 The boy did as he was told. Sure enough, a wonderful, two-stringed instrument was born. It is known as the *morin khurr,* which translates from Mongolian into English as "horse fiddle."

4 Interpret the clues in the image of the morin khurr. The decorations follow the horse's direction to the boy. The strings are made from horsehair. At the top of the fiddle, you will see a pegbox carved in the shape of a horse's head. The tuning pegs on either side are known as the "horse's ears."

COLLABORATE

Reread paragraphs 1 and 2. **Underline** what the horse tells the boy to do with his body. Discuss the text evidence that helps you know that legends such as this one contain fictional elements. Paraphrase the text evidence in your answer.

_____

_____

_____

_____

Reread paragraph 3. **Draw a box** around the words or phrases that tell what instrument was made.

A traditional morin khurr

nahariyani/Shutterstock.com

? **Why does the author address the reader in the closing paragraph?**

COLLABORATE

Talk About It Reread paragraph 4 on page 169. Analyze the photo of the horse fiddle. With a partner, talk about the ways in which the fiddle matches the description in the story.

Cite Text Evidence What text evidence shows that the morin khurr is based on the legend? Write the text evidence in the chart.

Detail

↓

Author's Purpose

Write The author addresses the reader in the closing paragraph because

_____

_____

_____

_____

Evaluate Information

A legend is a story passed down through the years. It is often based on real people or real events, but not everything in a legend is true, or possible. Analyze the setting and events that make this story a legend. How does the historical and cultural setting of this story affect the plot?

CHECK IN ▷ 1 ▷ 2 ▷ 3 ▷ 4

Similes and Metaphors

Figurative language includes similes and metaphors. Authors often use similes and metaphors to help their readers understand and picture ideas, as well as what is being described. A simile uses the words *like* or *as* to compare things. A metaphor makes a comparison without using the words *like* or *as*—for example, *she is a ray of sunshine.*

FIND TEXT EVIDENCE

On page 168 of "A Boy, a Horse, and a Fiddle" the author uses a simile in the second paragraph to help the readers picture the colt that the boy found.

> By a bush, he found a young colt, as white as snow, without its mother.

Your Turn Reread the last sentence of the first paragraph on **Literature Anthology** page 297.

- Is "the chieftain's face turned to stone" a simile or a metaphor? Explain your answer. _____

  _____

- Why do you think the author compares the chieftain's face to a stone?

  _____

  _____

Readers to Writers

Figurative language is a literary term. In figurative language, words are used in a different way than their usual, or literal, meaning. For example, in the metaphor *The sky is a blanket of stars*, the sky is being compared to a blanket of stars to create an image of a sky full of stars. A literal way to describe the sky could be, *There are many stars in the sky.* Think about how you use figurative and literal language in your own writing.

CHECK IN 1 2 3 4

? How do the poem, *A Window into History: The Mystery of the Cellar Window,* and "A Boy, a Horse, and a Fiddle" help you see the benefits of taking a second look?

COLLABORATE

Talk About It Read the poem. Talk with a partner about what the speaker does at the beginning of the poem and what the speaker does at the end.

Cite Text Evidence Work with a partner to **circle** ways the arrow and the song are similar. Then go back and illustrate by **making a mark** in the margin beside the lines that show how the speaker realizes that taking a second look is a good thing to do.

Write When they keep looking, the characters in the play and legend and the speaker of the poem discover

_____

_____

_____

_____

_____

Quick Tip

Talk about what the speaker in the poem discovers in the last stanza. How is that different from what happens in the first and second stanzas?

The Arrow and the Song

I shot an arrow into the air,
It fell to earth, I knew not where;
For, so swiftly it flew, the sight
Could not follow it in its flight.

I breathed a song into the air,
It fell to earth, I knew not where;
For who has sight so keen and strong,
That it can follow the flight of song?

Long, long afterward, in an oak
I found the arrow, still unbroke;
And the song, from beginning to end,
I found again in the heart of a friend.

—Henry Wadsworth Longfellow

CHECK IN 1 2 3 4

Plan a Time Capsule

What did you learn about giving things a second look from the characters you read about? Plan a time capsule in which you explain the significance of giving things a second look.

1 Look at your Build Knowledge notes in your reader's notebook.

2 Make a list of items you wish to include that represents what is important in your life today. Include at least three items. Use evidence from the texts to explain why it is important to give these items a second look.

3 Then write a paragraph explaining why you chose these items. Think about what meaningful message about life you would like to share with future generations. Use new vocabulary words.

Think about what you learned in this text set. Fill in the bars on page 151.

Build Knowledge

Essential Question

How do you express something that is important to you?

Build Vocabulary

Write new words you learned about the different ways we can express what is important to us. Draw lines and circles for the words you write.

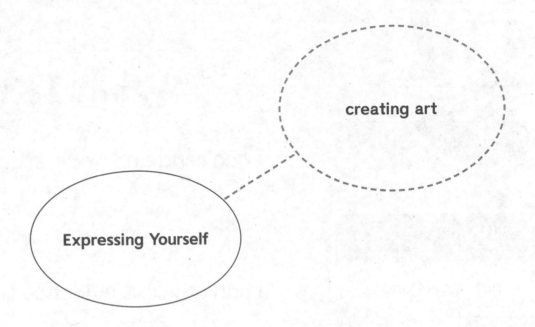

creating art

Expressing Yourself

Go online to **my.mheducation.com** and read the "Expressions of Freedom" Blast. Think about other symbols of hope and freedom. What would you do to express freedom? Then blast back your response.

MY GOALS

Think about what you already know. Fill in the bars. Let's keep learning!

What I Know Now

I can read and understand poetry.

1 > 2 > 3 > 4

I can use text evidence to respond to poetry.

1 > 2 > 3 > 4

I know there are many ways to express important ideas.

1 > 2 > 3 > 4

Key	
1 =	I do not understand.
2 =	I understand but need more practice.
3 =	I understand.
4 =	I understand and can teach someone.

 **STOP** You will come back to the next page later.

Think about what you learned. Fill in the bars. Keep working hard!

What I Learned

I can read and understand poetry.

1 2 3 4

I can use text evidence to respond to poetry.

1 2 3 4

I know there are many ways to express important ideas.

1 2 3 4

My Goal I can read and understand poetry.

TAKE NOTES

As you read, make note of interesting words and important details.

_____

_____

_____

_____

_____

_____

_____

_____

_____

_____

_____

_____

_____

_____

How Do I Hold the Summer?

The sun is setting sooner now,
My swimsuit's packed away.
How do I hold the summer fast,
Or ask it, please, to stay?

The lake like cold, forbidding glass—
The last sailboat has crossed.
Green leaves, gone gold, fall, float away—
Here's winter's veil of frost.

Essential Question

? How do you express something that is important to you?

Read three ways that poets express what matters to them.

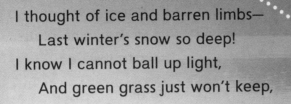

I thought of ice and barren limbs—
    Last winter's snow so deep!
I know I cannot ball up light,
    And green grass just won't keep,

So I'll search for signs of summer,
    Hold memories of each—
Soft plumes of brown pressed in a book,
    The pit of one ripe peach,

Each instance of a cricket's chirp,
    And every bird's sweet call,
And store them up in a poem to read
    When snow begins to fall.

— Maya Jones

(bkgd) Jean-Pierre Pieuchot/The Image Bank/Getty Images, (br) Robert Kirk/Photodisc/GettyImages

FIND TEXT EVIDENCE

Read

Page 178

Simile and Metaphor

Circle the line that makes a comparison about the lake. What two things are compared?

Page 178

Make Inferences

Why has the last sailboat crossed?

Page 179

Theme

Draw boxes around the sounds heard at the end of the poem. Why does the speaker mention these sounds?

Reread

Author's Craft

Do you think "How Do I Hold the Summer?" is a good title for this poem? Why or why not?

Read

Page 180

Alliteration

Circle the words that repeat beginning consonant sounds in the same line. What effect does this repetition have on the reader?

_____

_____

_____

Page 180

Theme

What is the poet's message about catching a fly?

_____

_____

_____

Reread

Author's Craft

Why did the poet use short lines to describe the action in the poem?

(t) Perry Hanson Concepts/Alamy; (bl) Stockbyte/Getty Images; (br) Noam Armonn/Alamy

Catching a Fly

It lighted, uninvited
upon the china plate
next to the peas.

No hand I raised
nor finger flicked
but rather found a lens

framed, focused,
zoomed in, held
the hands, still—

the appearance of hands,
like two fine threads, caught
plotting, planning—

greedy goggle eyes, webbed wings
like me, invading—
but no time to pause, he'd go—

and right at the last
instead of a swat,
I snapped!

— Ken Kines

WHEN I DANCE

Always wanna break out,
  use my arms and legs
    to shout!

On any dark day
  that doesn't go
    exactly my way—

I bust a move,
  get a groove,
    feet feel the ground—

That slap's
  the only sound
    slap, pound

my body needs to charge,
  I play my tracks,
    I make it large

to take myself away!
  Nothing else
    I need to say.

— T. C. Arcaro

Image courtesy of Tiffani Bearup/Flickr/Getty Images

Make Connections

Compare the forms of expression in the poems to the way you express what is important to you.

FIND TEXT EVIDENCE 🔍

Read

Page 181

Stanza and Meter

Draw a box around two sections that best express why dancing is important to the speaker. Explain your choice.

_____

_____

_____

_____

_____

_____

_____

_____

_____

_____

Reread

Author's Craft

How does the poet help you visualize what is expressed in the poem?

Vocabulary

Use the example sentences to talk with a partner about each word. Then answer the questions.

barren

The **barren** land did not have a single tree or bush.

What is another word or phrase for *barren*?

_____

_____

expression

James wrote songs as an **expression** of his thoughts about friendship.

Name another form of artistic expression.

_____

_____

meaningful

The students had a **meaningful** discussion about how to protect the environment.

What meaningful discussions have you had?

_____

_____

plumes

Each year, peacocks shed their beautiful tail **plumes** and grow new ones.

What beautiful plumes have you seen?

_____

_____

Poetry Terms

lyric

Some poets write **lyric** poetry that describes their feelings about nature and seasons.

Would you prefer to read a lyric poem about spring or fall?

_____

_____

alliteration

"Lou's lamb" shows **alliteration** because the same consonant sound begins two or more words.

Give another example of alliteration, using any consonant.

_____

_____

meter

Rita tapped her fingers in rhythm to the **meter** of the poem as she read it aloud.

Say the first line of *Jack and Jill* to yourself. What is the meter?

_____

_____

_____

stanza

In some poems, each **stanza** may have four lines.

How is a stanza like a paragraph?

_____

_____

_____

Build Your Word List Pick a word from any of the poems that you had a hard time pronouncing. A print or online dictionary can show you how to say the word. Write the word and its pronunciation and definition in your reader's notebook.

Simile and Metaphor

A **simile** makes a comparison using the words *like* or *as*: legs like sticks. A **metaphor** makes a comparison without using the words *like* or *as*: stick legs. These comparisons are figurative language because they are not used in a literal sense. Writers use them to create a vivid effect.

FIND TEXT EVIDENCE

The fifth stanza of "Catching a Fly" has the metaphor "greedy goggle eyes" that compares the fly's eyes to goggles, focused on food.

greedy goggle eyes, webbed wings
like me, invading—
but no time to pause, he'd go—

Your Turn Reread the fourth stanza of "Catching a Fly." What comparison does the simile make?

the appearance of hands,
like two fine threads, caught
plotting, planning—

_____

CHECK IN 1 2 3 4

Noam Armonn/Alamy Stock Photo

Stanza and Meter

A **stanza** is a section of the poem that expresses a key, or important, idea. Together these ideas help form a poem's main message. Poets may also use sound devices, such as **meter**, also called rhythm. In poetry, meter is a regular pattern of sounds in a line.

FIND TEXT EVIDENCE

Reread the poem "How Do I Hold the Summer?" on pages 178 and 179. Identify the stanzas in the poem, and think about how they are alike.

Page 179

So I'll search for signs of summer,
   Hold memories of each—
Soft plumes of brown pressed in a book,
   The pit of one ripe peach,

Each instance of a cricket's chirp,
   And every bird's sweet call,
And store them up in a poem to read
   When snow begins to fall.

Each stanza has four lines and contains a key idea.

An equal number of beats in the lines creates a regular meter, or rhythm.

Your Turn Identify the key idea of each stanza of "How Do I Hold the Summer?" How do these ideas help form the poem's main message?

_____

_____

_____

Quick Tip

A poem's title can give you many ideas about the poem. Think about the title of this poem. What images does it create? Does it tell you who or what the subject of the poem is? Does it give clues to the poem's main message?

CHECK IN   1   2   3   4

Lyric and Free Verse

Lyric poetry expresses personal thoughts and feelings. It often has a regular meter, or pattern of sounds. Lyric poetry may be arranged in stanzas and may contain rhyme and alliteration.

Free verse expresses ideas and feelings with carefully chosen words. It has no set rhyming pattern, meter, or line length. Free verse may include alliteration and stanzas.

FIND TEXT EVIDENCE

I can tell that "How Do I Hold the Summer?" is a lyric poem because it expresses the speaker's thoughts and feelings. It also includes rhyme, a regular meter, stanzas, and alliteration.

Page 178

How Do I Hold the Summer?

The sun is setting sooner now,
My swimsuit's packed away.
How do I hold the summer fast,
Or ask it, please, to stay?

The lake like cold, forbidding glass—
The last sailboat has crossed
Green leaves, gone gold, fall, float away—
Here's winter's veil of frost

Essential Question

How do you express something that is important to you?

Read three ways that poets express what matters to them.

The poem expresses feelings and includes rhyme.

The poem contains alliteration, with words that begin with the consonants g and f.

COLLABORATE

Your Turn Reread the poem "Catching a Fly" on page 180. Decide if it is an example of lyric or free verse poetry. What elements do you see?

_____

_____

_____

_____

CHECK IN 1 › 2 › 3 › 4

Theme

The **theme** of a poem is the message that the poet wishes to express. A poem can have multiple themes either stated directly or implied. Noticing poetic elements and important details can help you determine how a theme of a poem is developed.

 FIND TEXT EVIDENCE

All three poems have speakers who express something important to them, but each poem has a different theme. I'll reread "How Do I Hold the Summer?" and look for important details to determine a theme.

Quick Tip

A poem can have more than one theme. Another theme of "How Do I Hold the Summer?" is "Seasons don't last, but memories are forever." What other theme can you infer?

Detail
How do I hold the summer fast,   Or ask it, please, to stay?

↓

Detail
So I'll search for signs of summer,

↓

Detail
And store them up in a poem to read   When snow begins to fall.

↓

Theme
Good memories can be saved and revisited by recording our feelings about them in a poem.

 Your Turn Reread the poem "When I Dance." List key details in the graphic organizer on page 187. Use the details to figure out one theme of the poem.

CHECK IN 1 > 2 > 3 > 4

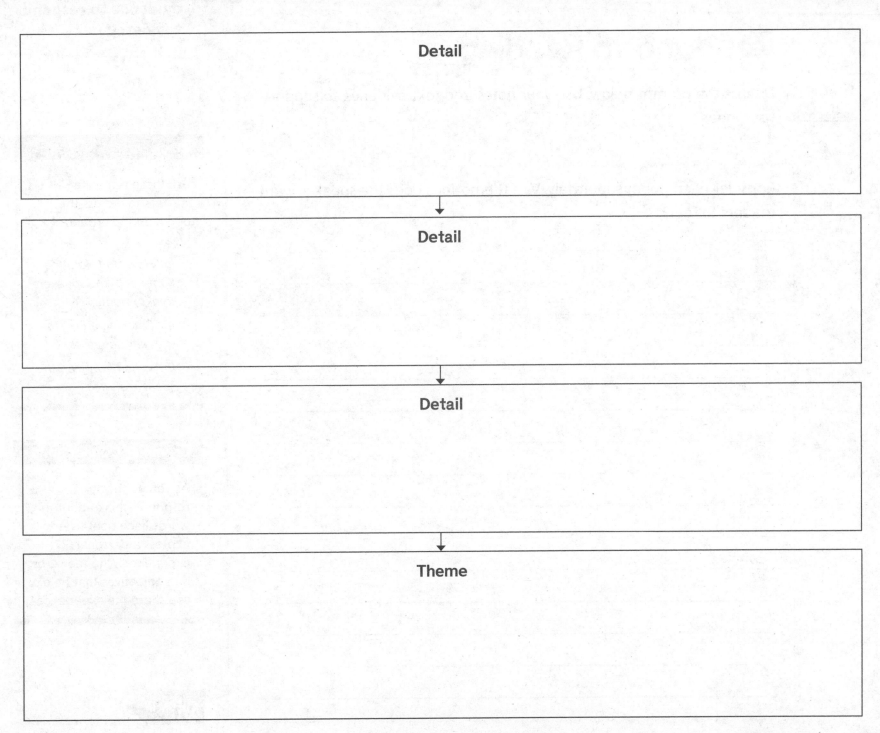

Detail

Detail

Detail

Theme

My Goal | **I can use text evidence to respond to poetry.**

Respond to Reading

COLLABORATE

Discuss the prompt below. Use your notes and text evidence to support your ideas.

Consider each poem separately. What emotions does the speaker want readers to feel?

_____

_____

_____

_____

_____

_____

_____

_____

_____

_____

_____

_____

_____

_____

_____

_____

Quick Tip

Use these sentence starters to discuss the poem and to organize ideas.

- In "How Do I Hold the Summer?," the speaker thinks about . . .

- In "Catching a Fly," the speaker describes . . .

- In "When I Dance," the speaker shares . . .

Grammar Connections

As you write your response, think about the words each poet uses to express a personal experience. Cite the verbs and adjectives that help you share the experience.

CHECK IN 1 2 3 4

What Is Important to You?

COLLABORATE

For many people, it is important to observe holidays. Research the origins and significance of the major national holidays in the United States. Then create a timeline. Work collaboratively with a larger group.

Step 1 **Set a Goal** Decide how you will research each holiday.

_____

Step 2 **Identify Sources** Discuss the print or online sources you will use.

Step 3 **Find and Record Information** First, identify if a source has relevant information. With a trusted adult, preview it before reading to see if it has information you need. Skim it quickly. Then read more carefully if you see information you might use.

As you quickly read through sources, how would you determine if the information is relevant to your topic?

_____

_____

Take notes and cite your sources. Research these questions:
- On what date did the holiday first become a national holiday?
- Who was the president who signed the bill that made it official?
- Why was it made a national holiday?

Step 4 **Organize and Synthesize Information** Plan what to include on your timeline and how you will create it.

Step 5 **Create and Present** Create your timeline. After you finish, present your work to the class.

Tech Tip

There are many websites that do not provide reliable information. Sometimes, the facts have not been checked. Usually, websites that end in .gov or .edu are good sites to gather information from.

National Holidays

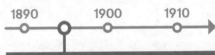

1890   1900   1910

LABOR DAY

June 28, 1894
Congress passed a bill; President Cleveland signed it into law.

The image above shows a part of a timeline about national holidays.

CHECK IN ⟩ 1 ⟩ 2 ⟩ 3 ⟩ 4

Words Free as Confetti

 How does the poet's use of free verse create the poem's mood?

Literature Anthology: pages 300–302

COLLABORATE

Talk About It Reread **Literature Anthology** page 300 out loud with a partner. Talk about how the poem makes you feel.

Cite Text Evidence What words and phrases does the poet use to create mood? Write text evidence in the chart below.

 Make Inferences

A poet carefully chooses what words or phrases to include in a poem. What inference can you make about why the poet includes Spanish words in the poem?

Text Evidence	How It Creates Mood

Write The poet uses free verse to create the poem's mood by _____

_____

_____

_____

CHECK IN 1 ⟩ 2 ⟩ 3 ⟩ 4

Dreams

In "Dreams," how does the poet use repetition and meter to help you understand his message?

Talk About It Reread **Literature Anthology** page 302. Turn to your partner, and discuss what you notice about the way the poem is organized and how that relates to the theme.

Cite Text Evidence What phrases are repeated, and how do they help the poet share his message? Write text evidence in the chart.

Text Evidence	Organization	Effect on Reader

Write The poet uses repetition and meter to _____

_____

_____

_____

Quick Tip

Look for phrases that are used more than once in the poem. These phrases may express the poet's message. Meter, also called rhythm, and repetition can work together to help you better understand the poem's theme.

Synthesize Information

What are the two things that Langston Hughes compares to dreams that die or are let go? What images and feelings do these things bring to mind? How do they help you understand the theme of the poem?

CHECK IN 1 2 3 4

Respond to Reading

My Goal

I can use text evidence to respond to poetry.

Discuss the prompt below. Use your notes and text evidence to support your response.

COLLABORATE

How does each poet's use of repetition and meter convey the theme of their poems?

_____

_____

_____

_____

_____

_____

_____

_____

_____

_____

_____

_____

_____

Quick Tip

Use these sentence starters to organize your text evidence.

• *In her poem, Pat Mora . . .*

• *Langston Hughes uses repetition to . . .*

• *This helps me understand the poets' messages because . . .*

CHECK IN ⟩ 1 ⟩ 2 ⟩ 3 ⟩ 4

A Story of How a Wall Stands

? How does the poet use dialogue to help you understand how the speaker's father feels about his work?

Literature Anthology: pages 304–305

Talk About It Reread **Literature Anthology** pages 304–305. Talk with a partner about how the speaker's father describes how he built a wall.

Cite Text Evidence What words and phrases help you figure out how the father feels about his work? Write evidence in the chart.

💡 Evaluate Information

Reread just the father's dialogue. Think about his words. How does his description of how he works add meaning to how a wall is built? What does this reveal about the speaker's father?

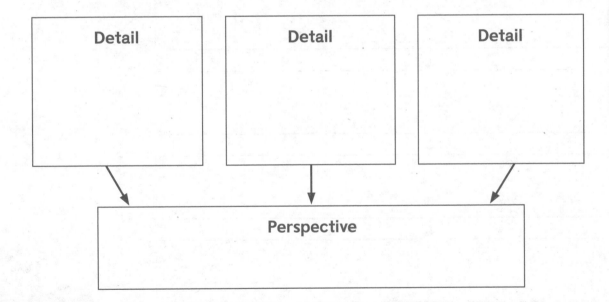

Detail	Detail	Detail

Perspective

Write The poet uses dialogue to show that the speaker's father feels _____

_____

_____

CHECK IN 1 2 3 4

? **Why does the poet suggest that stories are like a wall?**

Talk About It Reread the poem on **Literature Anthology** pages 304–305. With a partner, discuss what the poet wants readers to understand about this comparison.

Cite Text Evidence What words show how the poet feels about building a wall and building a story? Write text evidence in the chart.

Quick Tip

Reread the last stanza on page 305. Notice how the poet repeats the father's dialogue using the words "a long, long time." What does this repetition help emphasize?

How the Poet Feels

↓

↓

↓

Write The poet compares stories to a wall to show _____

_____

_____

Sascha/Photodisc/Getty Images

CHECK IN   1 > 2 > 3 > 4

Imagery

A poet uses **imagery** and figurative language to describe the speaker's feelings. To determine the speaker's feelings, analyze words and phrases that help create mental images or emphasize strong ideas. The poet's word choices, such as repetition, contribute to the speaker's voice. Voice is the speaker's specific personality.

 FIND TEXT EVIDENCE

In "A Story of How a Wall Stands" on pages 304-305 in the **Literature Anthology,** the speaker's father builds a stone wall as he explains to the speaker how he makes it strong. *Stone* is used many times in both the speaker's and the father's words. This imagery and repetition emphasize how much the speaker respects his father's strength.

COLLABORATE

Your Turn Reread the last stanza of the poem on page 305.

- What words are repeated in this stanza and from earlier in the poem?

  _____

- Identify examples of imagery and figurative language in this stanza. How do these elements deepen your understanding of the poem?

  _____

  _____

  _____

  _____

  _____

Readers to Writers

There are many ways to add voice to your writing, including repetition. Think about your feelings and attitude toward your topic. Choose words that express what you feel.

? How do the sculptors of this statue and the poets of "Words Free as Confetti" and "A Story of How a Wall Stands" express important ideas?

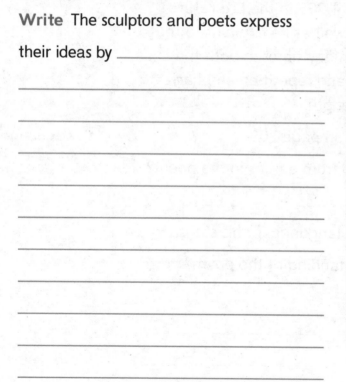
COLLABORATE

Talk About It Look at the photograph. Read the caption. With a partner, talk about how the sculptors expressed their ideas through art.

Cite Text Evidence **Draw boxes** around details in the photograph that tell you something about Abraham Lincoln. **Circle** clues that show the message the sculptors wanted to express.

Write The sculptors and poets express their ideas by _____

_____

_____

_____

_____

_____

_____

_____

Quick Tip

Feelings can be expressed in poetry or art, such as a sculpture. Think about how each poem is an expression of the poet. Then think about how the sculptors have expressed themselves.

This bronze statue depicts Abraham Lincoln and his horse, Old Bob, at the Lincoln Summer Home in Washington, D.C. It was created in 2009 by Ivan Schwartz, Stuart Williamson, and Jiwoong Cheh.

CHECK IN 1 2 3 4

Write a Poem

Think about the different ways you learned how to express what is important. Why is it significant that the poets you read use poetry to express important ideas?

1 Look at your Build Knowledge notes in your reader's notebook.

2 Think about how the poets describe what is important to them. Write down examples that helped you understand the emotions and feelings conveyed in the poems.

3 Write a poem that expresses an important idea. How would you convey your emotions and feelings in your poem? Would they be similar or different from those of the poets you read? Use new vocabulary words.

Think about what you learned in this text set. Fill in the bars on page 177.

Think about what you already know. Fill in the bars. It's important to keep learning.

Key	
1 =	I do not understand.
2 =	I understand but need more practice.
3 =	I understand.
4 =	I understand and can teach someone.

What I Know Now

I can write an expository essay.

1 > 2 > 3 > 4

I can synthesize information from four sources.

1 > 2 > 3 > 4

Think about what you learned. Fill in the bars. What helped you do your best?

What I Learned

I can write an expository essay.

1 2 3 4

I can synthesize information from four sources.

1 2 3 4

WRITING

WRITE TO SOURCES

You will answer an expository prompt using sources and a rubric.

ANALYZE THE RUBRIC

A rubric tells you what needs to be included in your writing.

Purpose, Focus, and Organization

Read the fifth bullet. Why is it important to state the central idea in the introduction?

_____

_____

_____

_____

Evidence and Elaboration

Read the second bullet. How is relevant evidence connected to the central idea?

_____

_____

_____

_____

Expository Writing Rubric

Purpose, Focus, and Organization • Score 4

- stays focused on the purpose, audience, and task
- clearly presents and fully develops the central idea about a topic
- uses transitional strategies, such as words and phrases, to connect ideas
- uses a logical text structure to organize information
- begins with a strong introduction and ends with a strong conclusion

Evidence and Elaboration • Score 4

- effectively supports the central idea with convincing facts and details
- **has strong examples of relevant evidence, or supporting details, from multiple sources**
- uses elaborative techniques, such as facts, examples, definitions, and quotations from sources
- expresses interesting ideas clearly using precise language
- uses appropriate academic and domain-specific language
- uses different sentence structures

Turn to page 240 for the complete Expository Writing Rubric.

Valentain Jevee/Shutterstock

Relevant Evidence and Sources

Use Multiple Sources Writers of expository essays do not rely on one source to find examples of relevant evidence. They draw upon multiple credible sources such as articles, essays, or books. Using multiple sources shows that the writer has found evidence from credible sources to strengthen the central idea. Read the paragraph below.

> May Mann Jennings was more than the wife of Florida's governor, William Jennings. She was a prominent Florida activist, suffragist, and a champion of environmental causes. She helped create the Royal Palm State Park that would later become a part of the Everglades. According to the article "Florida's National Forests" this park was successfully created in 1916. It was the first Florida state park to be created. But she was determined to protect other forests in Florida, says the article "May Jennings: A Life." In 1927, she helped promote the legislative act to create the Florida State Board of Forestry. For her conservation work, Jennings is called the Mother of Florida Forestry.

What is the central idea of this paragraph? How does the evidence from the sources support it?

_____

_____

_____

_____

WRITING

ANALYZE THE STUDENT MODEL

Paragraphs 1–2

Circle the central idea in paragraph 1. Read paragraph 2. A supporting detail is highlighted. **Underline** another example of a supporting detail in paragraph 2. What can you infer about Warren's education from the details in paragraph 2?

_____

_____

_____

_____

Paragraph 3

Draw a box around a transition that links paragraph 2 to paragraph 3. What evidence does Jacob include to show what Mitchell wanted to change?

_____

_____

_____

Jacob responded to the writing prompt: *Write an expository essay to present to your class about how women worked to improve government and society*. Read Jacob's essay below.

1   It's hard to believe that at one time our country didn't let women own property, vote, or get an education. Despite those obstacles, women still managed to fight for women's rights and other reforms.

2   It was 1775, and British soldiers occupied Boston. Mercy Otis Warren decided to fight back. According to "Weighing in with Words," she wrote popular plays that mocked the British. Because she was a woman, Warren had to publish her plays anonymously. It wasn't until 1790 that Warren published plays under her own name. In her writing, Warren argued that women should be able to participate in public affairs.

3   Another woman who fought for women's rights was Maria Mitchell. Mitchell was born on Nantucket Island in 1818. Her father taught her astronomy because her parents believed in educating boys and girls. In 1865, Vassar, a women's college, hired Mitchell as an astronomy professor. At that time, people thought that education made girls sick and unfeminine. During her career, Mitchell gave many lectures about a woman's right to an education.

4 Jane Addams fought for people who had few or no rights. She is famous for cofounding Hull House in 1889, a place that provided education and support for immigrant families in Chicago. The article "Democracy, One Step at a Time" explains how in 1912, Addams helped to write Theodore Roosevelt's party platform when Roosevelt was running for a third term as president. His party supported child labor reform and women's suffrage. However, since she was a woman, Addams couldn't even vote for him!

5 Women finally did get the vote in 1920. Two women named Elizabeth Cady Stanton and Susan B. Anthony spent most of their lives fighting for women's rights, especially the right to vote. As a young girl, Stanton remembered women coming to see her father, a lawyer. Since married women weren't allowed to own property or vote, her father couldn't help them. Stanton said that this "drew my attention to the injustice and cruelty of the laws." Her father encouraged her to work to change the laws.

6 Throughout history, women have worked for reforms and equal rights. Many women did this at a time when they had few, if any, rights themselves. Yet they never stopped fighting.

Paragraph 4

Draw a box around the source that Jacob uses. **Circle** an example of end punctuation that varies Jacob's sentence structure. What is an example of elaboration that Jacob uses in the same paragraph?

_____

_____

_____

_____

_____

Paragraphs 4–5

What text structure does Jacob use to organize his information?

_____

_____

Paragraph 6

Underline the sentence in the conclusion that restates Jacob's central idea from paragraph 1.

Apply the Rubric

With a partner, use the rubric on page 200 to discuss why Jacob scored a 4 on his essay.

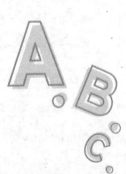

My Goal: I can write an expository essay.

Analyze the Prompt

Writing Prompt

Write an expository essay to explain to your class about how people spoke up for civil rights.

Purpose, Audience, and Task Reread the writing prompt. What is your purpose for writing? My purpose is to _____

_____

Who will your audience be? My audience will be _____

_____

What type of writing is the prompt asking for? _____

_____

Set a Purpose for Reading Sources Asking questions about civil rights will help you figure out your purpose for reading. You will read a passage set about how people spoke up for civil rights. The fourth source in the passage set will be "Our Voices, Our Votes" on pages 280–283 in the **Literature Anthology**. Before you read the passage set about civil rights activists, write a question here.

_____

_____

_____

Read the following passage set.

BUILDING A BETTER WORLD

SOURCE 1

1   Mary McLeod Bethune was an educator and a women's and civil rights activist. In her lifetime, Bethune taught and ran educational institutions for a total of forty-five years. She believed that education was important for empowering women and for supporting the civil rights movement.

2   Bethune started her first school in a house in Daytona Beach, Florida. At the time, there were no schools for black girls. Her school was so successful that it outgrew the house. She purchased land to build a bigger school. This new school opened in 1904. Bethune continued to support it. She raised money door-to-door and asked businesses for donations. In 1929, it merged with the all-boys Cookman Institute and became a college, accepting boys and girls. Today, the school is called Bethune-Cookman University, and is still active.

3   In 1936, President Franklin Roosevelt appointed her director of the Division of Negro Affairs of the National Youth Administration (NYA). She was the first African American to lead a federal agency. She worked with federal and state organizations to support the rights of African American youth. Then, at the start of World War II, Bethune counseled Roosevelt about allowing African American women to serve in the European conflict.

4   After leaving the NYA, Bethune returned to Bethune-Cookman College. She lived there until she died in 1955. Through her teaching experience and leadership, she changed the lives of many women and men. Her life and efforts were honored with a memorial statue in 1974 and a postage stamp in 1985.

EXPOSITORY ESSAY

FIND TEXT EVIDENCE

Paragraph 1
The central idea is highlighted. What does the central idea tell you about the focus of the source?

_____

_____

Paragraph 2
What facts and details support the central idea?

_____

_____

_____

Paragraphs 3–4
Circle the ways Bethune used her voice in government. Then underline the ways she was honored for her leadership.

Take Notes Paraphrase the central idea of the source, and give examples of supporting details.

WRITING

FIND TEXT EVIDENCE

Paragraph 5

What is the central idea of this source?

_____

_____

Paragraph 6

Circle the ways Truth used her voice to speak out against mistreatment of African Americans.

Paragraphs 7–8

The author gives an exact date of a specific event. This detail has been highlighted. Why is this date important, and why does the author include this detail?

_____

_____

_____

_____

Take Notes Paraphrase the central idea of the source, and give examples of supporting details.

SOURCE 2

THE POWER OF Words

5   For centuries, women were often only recognized for their roles as wives and mothers. Their voices were not expected to be heard beyond their families and homes. In nineteenth-century (1801–1900) America, this idea began to change. Women found their voice. They began to gain power as speakers and activists. In fact, several powerful women were responsible for bringing about positive change.

6   Sojourner Truth is one of the most famous women known for speaking up during the 1800s. Truth was born into slavery in 1797. She escaped to freedom in 1826, but still lived in a time where African Americans and women were treated poorly. Truth traveled around the nation, preaching and protesting slavery. In 1850, she dictated her autobiography. Her book was a huge success and earned her national acclaim. As a former enslaved woman, her words inspired many people.

7   The twentieth century (1901–2000) brought about more positive change. More women spoke up, including Clara Lemlich. Lemlich organized several worker strikes, since factory conditions were terrible. On November 22, 1909, Lemlich spoke in front of a crowd of factory workers. As a result, thousands of people protested in the streets. After two months, factory owners agreed to better pay and shorter workdays.

8   Many women inspired positive change in the nineteenth and twentieth centuries. They traveled around America and gave influential speeches. These speeches excited and inspired crowds of people. They often pointed out that inequality existed between races and genders. Their powerful words are still praised today.

"Democracy's Limits" by Eric Arnesen, *Cobblestone*, 4/1/2018 © by Carus Publishing Company. Reproduced with permission. All Cricket Media material is copyrighted by Carus Publishing Company, d/b/a Cricket Media, and/or various authors and illustrators. Any commercial use or distribution of material without permission is strictly prohibited. Please visit http://www.cricketmedia.com/licensing for licensing and http://www.cricketmedia.com for subscriptions.
Thomas D. McAvoy/The LIFE Picture Collection/Getty Imagea

A War at HOME and ABROAD

9   The fight for equal rights has long been a part of America's military history. During World War II (1939–1945), African American citizens in many parts of the country could not serve in some branches of the military. According to activist A. Philip Randolph, all Americans wanted an equal role in the war, no matter the color of their skin. Randolph fought for civil rights. He demanded that the government integrate the armed forces.

10   As the war continued, racial tension in the United States grew. In September 1940, Randolph met with President Franklin D. Roosevelt and demanded the integration of the armed forces. Roosevelt did not act. As a result, Randolph organized a different approach.

11   In January 1941, Randolph created the March on Washington movement. This event aimed to bring citizens together to protest racial inequality in Washington, D.C. The expected number of participants grew from ten thousand to a hundred thousand people. Facing growing pressure, President Roosevelt signed Executive Order 8802 in June, later that year. This law declared, "There shall be no discrimination in the employment of workers in defense industries or government because of race, creed, color, or national origin."

12   Despite this victory, the armed forces remained segregated. It would be another seven years before President Harry S. Truman issued Executive Order 9981, which finally integrated the armed forces. Randolph was just one of the many activists who fought for civil rights during World War II.

EXPOSITORY ESSAY

FIND TEXT EVIDENCE

Paragraph 9
Circle the central idea.

Paragraphs 9–10
Reread the title and these paragraphs. Why is this a good title for this text?

_____

_____

_____

_____

Paragraphs 11–12
What is the difference between Executive Order 8802 and Executive Order 9981?

_____

_____

_____

_____

Take Notes Paraphrase the central idea of the source and give examples of supporting details.

My Goal I can synthesize information from four sources.

TAKE NOTES

Read the writing prompt below. Then use the four sources, your notes, and the graphic organizer to plan a response.

Writing Prompt *Write an expository essay to explain to your class about how people spoke up for civil rights.*

Synthesize Information

Review the evidence recorded from each source. How does the information show how people spoke up for civil rights? Discuss your ideas with a partner.

CHECK IN 1 > 2 > 3 > 4 >

Plan: Organize Ideas

Central Idea	Supporting Ideas
People spoke up for equality by fighting for fair and just treatment.	People figured out how to solve unfair treatment.

Relevant Evidence

Source 1	Source 2	Source 3	Source 4
Because there was no school for black girls, Bethune opened her own school. She believed that education was important to empowerment.	Lemlich spoke out against horrible factory conditions. Her speech led workers to protest, and eventually the factory owners agreed to better pay and shorter hours.		

(bkgd) Valentain Jevee/Shutterstock

Draft: Strong Introduction

Introduce Your Topic Writers of expository texts carefully consider what to include in their introduction. A strong introduction can start with facts, anecdotes, questions, or quotations to grab the reader's attention. It provides the reader with enough relevant background information. Most importantly, it clearly states the central idea about a topic. It does not include unnecessary details.

Read the example below. Then revise it by deleting unnecessary ideas to make a strong, clear introduction.

> In 1951, eight-year-old Linda Brown was the subject of the Brown v. Board of Education civil rights case. She wasn't allowed to attend a school near her home. Instead, she was forced to attend another school that was far away. To get to school, Linda had to walk to the bus stop. She had to wait for the bus. She had to ride the bus.

_____

_____

_____

_____

Draft Use your graphic organizer and the example above to write your draft in your writer's notebook. Before you start writing, review the rubric on page 200. Remember to indent each paragraph.

Grammar Connections

As you write your draft, use correct subject-verb agreement with indefinite pronouns. Look at the phrase that follows the pronoun to decide whether to use a singular or plural verb: *All of the sky is blue. All of the stories are important.*

CHECK IN 1 2 3 4

Revise: Peer Conferences

Review a Draft Listen actively to your partner. Take notes about what you liked and what was difficult to follow. Begin by telling what you liked. Use these sentence starters.

Your introduction grabbed my attention because . . .
Can you clarify what you meant by . . .
I think adding another source can help to . . .

After you finish giving each other feedback, reflect on the peer conference. What suggestion did you find to be the most helpful?

Revision Use the Revising Checklist to help you figure out what text you may need to move, elaborate on, or delete. After you finish writing your final draft, use the full rubric on pages 240–243 to score your essay.

Next, you'll write an expository essay on a new topic.

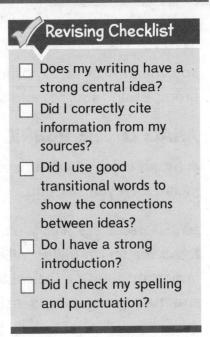

My Score			
Purpose, Focus, & Organization (4 pts)	Evidence & Elaboration (4 pts)	Conventions (2 pts)	Total (10 pts)

WRITE TO SOURCES

You will answer an expository prompt using sources and a rubric.

ANALYZE THE RUBRIC

A rubric tells you what needs to be included in your writing.

Purpose, Focus, and Organization

Read the fourth bullet. Why is it important to use a logical text structure to organize ideas?

_____

_____

_____

Evidence and Elaboration

Read the third bullet. How does using elaborative techniques such as quotations and definitions support a central idea?

_____

_____

_____

_____

_____

Expository Writing Rubric

Purpose, Focus, and Organization • Score 4

- stays focused on the purpose, audience, and task
- clearly presents and fully develops the central idea about a topic
- uses transitional strategies, such as words and phrases, to connect ideas
- **uses a logical text structure to organize information**
- begins with a strong introduction and ends with a strong conclusion

Evidence and Elaboration • Score 4

- effectively supports the central idea with convincing facts and details
- has strong examples of relevant evidence, or supporting details, from multiple sources
- uses elaborative techniques, such as facts, examples, definitions, and quotations from sources
- expresses interesting ideas clearly using precise language
- uses appropriate academic and domain-specific language
- uses different sentence structures

Turn to page 240 for the complete Expository Writing Rubric.

Logical Text Structure

Organize Ideas When authors plan their ideas, they think about how to structure their writing so that it makes logical sense. For example, an author who writes informational texts about historical figures may organize ideas in a logical structure, such as a sequence of events. Similarly, an author writing about two artists' works might use a comparison-and-contrast structure to show the similarities and differences.

> Martha Graham was one of the twentieth century's most important dancers. She was the first to create bold, expressive movements. In the early 1920s, Graham danced professionally before teaching dance at various schools. Then in 1926, Graham started her own dance school. Her school was so successful that it expanded into a large dance company. Over time, students joined other studios that followed Graham's groundbreaking style. Graham danced until she was in her mid-seventies and choreographed until she died at age ninety-six. Today, her company still creates new dances that capture her spirit.

Read the paragraph above. How is the information in this paragraph organized? Cite text evidence.

_____

_____

_____

_____

_____

Audience

Strong writers think about their audience. If the events in their essay are presented in an order that does not make sense, they might confuse their readers. Pay close attention to words that show a sequence of events. Phrases that include dates help link a sequence of events. Transitional words such as *eventually*, *recently*, and *later* also show a logical sequence.

WRITING

ANALYZE THE STUDENT MODEL

Paragraph 1

Circle the central idea in paragraph 1.

Paragraph 2

Underline an example of a supporting detail in paragraph 2.

Paragraphs 2-3

Write down an example of a transitional word or phrase that connects paragraph 2 with paragraph 3.

_____

_____

What can you infer about how the poet Paul Laurence Dunbar feels about the arrival of spring from the details in paragraphs 2 and 3?

_____

_____

_____

_____

Student Model: Expository Text

Gabrielle responded to the writing prompt: *Write an expository essay to present to your class about how nature inspires poets.* Read Gabrielle's essay below.

1   Anyone who has had to write a story or a poem knows how hard it is to think of an idea. Many writers get their ideas from nature. Poets especially like to write about nature. They often use elements of nature like flowers or the change of seasons as a metaphor or a symbol for a bigger idea.

2   The poet Paul Laurence Dunbar was inspired to write poems about spring, summer, fall, and winter. According to the source "Seasons as Symbols," winter stands for old age, while spring makes people think of new beginnings. Dunbar wrote about spring in his poem "Spring Song."

        Sweet perfumes scent the balmy air,

        And life is brimming everywhere.

3   Flowers start blooming in the spring, and Dunbar talks about how sweet the flowers smell. Winter is now over. The weather gets warmer, and trees grow leaves. Everything comes back to life after winter ends. The exclamation point that Dunbar uses shows the idea that life is everywhere—for example, "Spring, Spring, Spring!" I think it makes the line more joyful, as though the poet shouts his happiness.

4   Along with the change of seasons, flowers are another popular subject for poets. Everyone knows that a red rose stands for love. However, did you know that people used to communicate using flowers? In the article "The Language of Flowers," the author says that in the eighteenth and nineteenth centuries, each flower had a special meaning. The nineteenth-century poet Emily Dickinson often used flowers in her poems. In one poem, Dickinson writes about a daisy. In "The Language of Flowers," a daisy means innocence.

             So has a Daisy vanished

             From the fields today.

5   The poem is not just about a daisy disappearing from a field. The daisy also represents the loss of someone who was innocent. Also, according to the article "The Language of Flowers," the name Daisy was popular in the nineteenth century. Dickinson capitalized "Daisy" in the poem, so she may have been writing about a real person.

6   One reason Dickinson was inspired by plants was that she studied botany, the science of plants. According to the article "Emily's Book," Dickinson dried and pressed over four hundred plants. So, the next time you need an idea for a poem or a story, take a walk outside and get inspired by nature!

EXPOSITORY ESSAY

Paragraph 4

Draw boxes around the sources that Gabrielle uses.

What is an example of elaboration that Gabrielle uses in the same paragraph?

_____

_____

_____

Paragraph 5

What text structure does Gabrielle use to organize the information in her essay?

_____

_____

Paragraph 6

Underline the sentence in the conclusion that restates Gabrielle's central idea from paragraph 1.

Apply the Rubric

With a partner, use the rubric on page 212 to discuss why Gabrielle scored a 4 on her essay.

Analyze the Prompt

Writing Prompt

Write an expository essay to explain to your class about how writers and artists express their opinions and perspectives.

Purpose, Audience, and Task Reread the writing prompt. What is your purpose for writing? My purpose is to _____

_____

Who will your audience be? My audience will be _____

_____

What type of writing is the prompt asking for? _____

_____

Set a Purpose for Reading Sources Asking questions about what inspires writers and artists to express their opinions and perspectives will help you figure out your purpose for reading. Before you read the passage set about writers' and artists' works, write a question here.

_____

_____

_____

Read the following passage set.

A LIFE IN *Color*

1   Mario Sanchez was a folk artist who lived in Key West, Florida. Born in 1908, Sanchez was a self-taught artist who mainly lived in the lively neighborhood of Gato's Village. Although he began drawing on items like paper grocery bags, Sanchez became famous for his painted wood carvings that depicted street scenes and everyday Floridian life. He used bright paint colors to depict the colorful community he saw.

2   Sanchez's family had immigrated to Florida from Cuba in the late 1880s. His family was very popular in their Key West neighborhood. His grandfather owned a grocery store on a street corner, which locals called Sanchez Corner. Mario Sanchez was inspired by his family's rich history and the events he witnessed as a child in this community. His art shows people dancing and gossiping outside of local buildings and on docks. He used his art to depict Florida life as he saw it.

3   Sanchez once said, "We like to talk about our heritage. We were taught to appreciate our ancestors. Every generation should tell the next one about its ancestors." Sanchez is considered a "memory artist" because his works serve as an accurate snapshot of daily life in a busy seaside neighborhood in the 1900s. When we look at his carvings, we can see the streets of his childhood. Mario Sanchez is considered one of the most important Cuban American folk artists of the twentieth century.

Twenty Five December/Shutterstock

EXPOSITORY ESSAY

FIND TEXT EVIDENCE

Paragraph 1
Read the highlighted central idea in paragraph 1.

Paragraph 2
What influenced Sanchez to create everyday scenes in his art? **Draw a box** around this detail.

Paragraph 3
The author cites Sanchez's own words. **Underline** these words or quotation.

How is this quotation an example of elaboration?

_____

_____

_____

_____

_____

_____

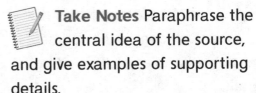 **Take Notes** Paraphrase the central idea of the source, and give examples of supporting details.

Paragraph 4
Circle examples of strong language that reinforces the central idea.

Paragraph 5
A detail has been highlighted. How does this detail support the central idea?

_____

_____

_____

Paragraph 6
What text structure does the author use to organize this passage?

_____

_____

_____

✏️ **Take Notes** Paraphrase the central idea of the source, and give examples of supporting details.

THE FEDERAL ART PROJECT

4   The Federal Art Project (FAP) was a government program created in 1935. Its goal was to help sustain artists during the Great Depression. Formed under President Franklin D. Roosevelt's New Deal, the FAP funded art programs. It built community centers that hosted shows and offered classes. It hired thousands of artists. Indeed, FAP inspired people to find new ways to express and support themselves during a time when many were struggling.

5   FAP was established as part of the larger Works Progress Administration (WPA). Over the eight years it existed, the WPA hired as many as ten thousand artists to create paintings, murals, and posters across the country. The WPA itself funded 125,000 new buildings, including over 100 community art centers. These projects were massive in scale, and they required a lot of workers and painters. **In total, the WPA helped 8.5 million Americans earn wages.**

6   Then the community centers came up with a way to share event information with the public. Over two thousand posters were created under FAP. They helped spread the word about new community events, shows, and even health and educational programs. FAP hired artists to create these posters. These new programs inspired people to learn about art and education. Struggling artists now had a way to support themselves. The public also had a new appreciation for art. Many Americans benefited from FAP during the Great Depression.

William Bartram:
One With Nature

7   William Bartram (1739–1823) was a traveler, naturalist, and writer who explored the eastern coast in the 1700s of what is now the United States. Although he was born in Philadelphia, Pennsylvania, his most famous work is based on his experiences of what is Florida today. His work is remarkable because it combines science, art, and a respect for nature into something new and completely his own.

8   In 1773, Bartram was hired to explore sections of Florida, and Bartram did just that. As he explored, he recorded his experiences. His explorations inspired him to write about the landscapes he saw. His writings were later made into a book called *Travels*. In the book, Bartram describes traveling up the St. Johns River to present-day Blue Spring and Astor. *Travels* was considered one of the most prized scientific books of the time.

9   Bartram is remembered and praised for his efforts to record the many plants and animals he encountered. He used vivid imagery and detailed illustrations in his descriptions. Bartram is considered "the first naturalist who penetrated the dense tropical forests of Florida." Present-day scientists continue to study his work. Florida even has a highway named after him: the William Bartram Scenic and Historic Highway. The road runs along the east side of the same river he traveled hundreds of years ago.

FIND TEXT EVIDENCE 🔍

Paragraph 7
What facts and details does the author use to introduce Bartram? **Underline** them.

Paragraph 8
Draw a box around the source the author includes in this paragraph.

Paragraph 9
In the conclusion, the author gives a quotation. **Paraphrase** it.

_____

_____

_____

What lasting impression does Bartram's work have on people today? Cite text evidence.

_____

_____

_____

✎ **Take Notes** Paraphrase the central idea of the source, and give examples of supporting details.

Natalya Chernyavskaya/Shutterstock

My Goal I can synthesize information from three sources.

TAKE NOTES

Read the writing prompt below. Then use the three sources, your notes, and the graphic organizer to plan a response.

Writing Prompt *Write an expository essay to explain to your class about how writers and artists express their opinions and perspectives.*

Synthesize Information

Review the evidence recorded from each source. How does the information show how writers and artists express their opinions and pespectives? Discuss your ideas with a partner.

CHECK IN 1 > 2 > 3 > 4 >

Plan: Organize Ideas

Central Idea	Supporting Ideas
Writers and artists used their work to make a statement about the community and the culture they lived in.	Writers and artists created art to depict details of everyday life in their community.

Relevant Evidence

Source 1	Source 2	Source 3
Sanchez used art to depict everyday scenes of his family, their culture, and their home in Key West.	FAP artists created posters to depict community events and even health information that would benefit many people.	

Draft: Strong Conclusion

End With an Effective Conclusion An expository essay may end with a conclusion that restates the central idea. When you conclude your essay, refer back to your introduction, sum up the details, and end it with a final observation, message, or thought. Read the paragraph below. Then revise it to improve sentence structure by deleting unnecessary ideas to make a strong, clear conclusion.

Grammar Connections

As you write, make sure your pronouns and antecedents are in agreement. For example, you wouldn't write: "He delivered their speech." You would write, "He delivered his speech."

> In the early 1900s, writers and activists Booker T. Washington and W.E.B. Du Bois disagreed on how to confront racism in the United States. During the 1930s, poets such as Langston Hughes and Gwendolyn Brooks spoke out against racial discrimination. These writers inspired other people to stand up for what they believed in. Their writing also inspired them to stand up for what they felt was right. These are the reasons that these writers are honored and remembered.

_____

_____

_____

_____

Draft Use your graphic organizer and the information above to write your draft in your writer's notebook. Before you start writing, review the rubric on page 212. Remember to indent each paragraph.

CHECK IN 1 2 3 4

Revise: Peer Conferences

Review a Draft Listen actively to your partner. Take notes about what you liked and what was difficult to follow. Begin by telling what you liked. Use these sentence starters.

Your conclusion made me excited to read more about . . .
Your text structure is clear because . . .
I think adding another detail can help to . . .

After you finish giving each other feedback, reflect on the peer conference. What suggestion did you find to be the most helpful?

_____

_____

_____

Revision Use the Revising Checklist to help you figure out what text you may need to move, elaborate on, or delete. After you finish writing your final draft, use the full rubric on pages 240–243 to score your essay.

Revising Checklist

- [ ] Does my writing have a strong central idea?
- [ ] Did I include enough relevant evidence to support my central idea?
- [ ] Are all ideas structured in a logical order, or do I need to rearrange details?
- [ ] Do I have a strong conclusion?
- [ ] Did I check my spelling and punctuation?

Turn to page 199. Fill in the bars to show what you learned.

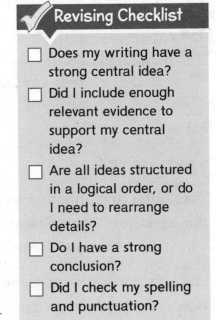

My Score			
Purpose, Focus, & Organization (4 pts)	Evidence & Elaboration (4 pts)	Conventions (2 pts)	Total (10 pts)

TAKE NOTES

Take notes and annotate as you read the passages "Cesar Chavez: Hero at Work" and "Army of Helpers."

Look for the answer to the question: *How can people make positive contributions to society?*

_____

_____

_____

_____

_____

_____

_____

_____

_____

_____

_____

PASSAGE 1 BIOGRAPHY

CESAR CHAVEZ: Hero at Work

In 1965, Chavez asked people to boycott grapes to get growers to set safe standards for pesticide use.

Some people have devoted their lives to making the world a better place, and Cesar Chavez was one of them.

Cesar Estrada Chavez was born to a farming family in Yuma, Arizona, on March 31, 1927. In 1938, a drought hit. The Chavez family lost their farm and headed for California. His parents became migrant workers. They traveled from one job to the next, working on farms and ranches. Cesar had to stop going to school after eighth grade to help in the fields. He spent long hours in harsh conditions, bent over in the hot sun. The workers received low pay. They lived in camps with unclean water and insect infestations. He and others were exposed to harmful pesticides, which are substances that kill pests, such as plant-eating insects.

Chavez served in the US Navy during World War II. After returning to the fields, he became involved with efforts to improve conditions. In 1962, he helped found a labor union, along with another leader named Dolores Huerta, called the National Farm Workers Association (NFWA). Chavez led protests and strikes, which are refusals to work, to call attention to the workers' issues. In the 1960s, he got people across America to boycott, or stop buying, California grapes to protest conditions on farms. In 1968, he went to Congress to talk about the effects of pesticides on people's health.

In 1971, the NFWA became the United Farm Workers (UFW). The UFW won higher pay and benefits for its members. Some of the unhealthful pesticides were outlawed. After thirty years fighting for better conditions, Chavez died on April 23, 1993. He is remembered by many as a hero of working people.

ARMY of Helpers

I will get things done for America to make our people safer, smarter, and healthier.

—from the AmeriCorps pledge

Since 1994, thousands of Americans have taken the AmeriCorps pledge to serve their nation. The US government, along with other organizations interested in building stronger communities, provides funding for AmeriCorps. The people in this volunteer army help with health care, public safety, the environment, and education.

TAKE NOTES

Jim West/Alamy Stock Photo; (border) McGraw-Hill Education

TAKE NOTES

Across the country, team members save lives by teaching the benefits of healthful living. Volunteers work in city health clinics, for instance, to help poor families connect to health services. They also sign people up for disease-prevention programs.

AmeriCorps forms its teams based on need. Volunteers age seventeen or older serve for three months to a year. Full-time workers may sign up to get some money during their service, but most sign up for the experience. Disaster-response teams often travel to areas hit by hurricanes and other natural disasters. They provide disease-stopping sanitation and other aid. "Best year of my life!" said one volunteer on the group's social media page.

Social media shows the group's workers delivering nutritious meals to people battling disease, volunteers coaching students on how to address bullies, and more. AmeriCorps also provides online resources with public safety information, such as storm alerts. But the real work happens in person, in service to others in need.

Andy Cross/Contributor/Getty Images

COMPARE THE PASSAGES

Review your notes from "Cesar Chavez: Hero at Work" and "Army of Helpers." Note the ways the people in these texts make positive contributions to society. Then identify the central idea you learned by reading both texts.

Cesar Chavez: Hero at Work	Army of Helpers

Central Idea I Learned

💡 Synthesize Information

Think about both texts. Why is it significant that people contribute to society in different ways? Write your ideas in your reader's notebook.

CHECK IN 1 2 3 4

ANALYZE A QUOTE

> "Ask not what your country can do for you—ask what you can do for your country."
>
> —John F. Kennedy, thirty-fifth US President

What does the Kennedy quote mean? Think about things people do for their country. Then write about this topic. Use at least one fact from "Cesar Chavez: Hero at Work" and at least one fact from "Army of Helpers" in your response. Use five words from the WORD BOX below.

Kennedy speaks at his presidential inauguration, 1961.

WORD BOX

advocate	aid	assist	defend	engage
help	obey	organize	participate	pay
pledge	promise	protect	respect	serve
support	uphold	volunteer	vote	

_____

_____

_____

_____

_____

_____

CREATE A BROCHURE

With a partner, research an organization that has made positive contributions to society. You and your partner will create a brochure that presents and summarizes the information. After you complete your brochure, you will present it to your class.

First, think about how the organization helps other people. What kind of work does the organization do? For example, does the organization improve living or working conditions? Or does it raise awareness about important social issues?

Then gather information from reliable print or digital sources. After you've completed your research, remember to cite the sources you've used.

Finally, plan what to include in your brochure, such as photos and captions. If possible, you may use computer software programs to help you design your brochure.

Write your notes on the lines below.

_____

_____

_____

_____

_____

_____

_____

My Goal I can read and understand science texts.

TAKE NOTES

Take notes and annotate as you read the passages "Colorful Chameleons" and "Changing Their Look."

Look for the answer to the question: *Why is camouflage important to animals' survival?*

_____

_____

_____

_____

_____

_____

_____

_____

_____

_____

_____

_____

PASSAGE 1 EXPOSITORY TEXT

Colorful Chameleons

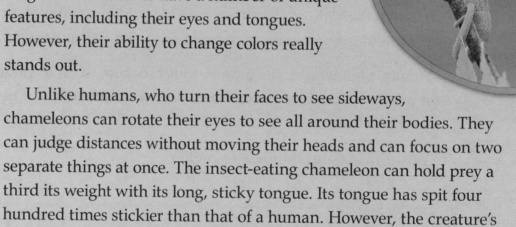

About half of all chameleon species are found in trees in Madagascar, an island nation off the southeast coast of Africa. The largest chameleon reaches 23 inches (60 cm) in length. The smallest is just under 0.9 inches (2.54 cm) long. These creatures have a number of unique features, including their eyes and tongues. However, their ability to change colors really stands out.

Unlike humans, who turn their faces to see sideways, chameleons can rotate their eyes to see all around their bodies. They can judge distances without moving their heads and can focus on two separate things at once. The insect-eating chameleon can hold prey a third its weight with its long, sticky tongue. Its tongue has spit four hundred times stickier than that of a human. However, the creature's most striking feature is probably its color-changing powers.

Human skin usually grows darker when exposed to sunlight because of pigments inside the lowest layer of skin cells. Animals like the squid change color by sending pigments through their cells. Chameleons change color in a different process. They have specially structured skin cells that reflect light to change hue.

How? Imagine a chameleon relaxing on a branch, with its skin relaxed, when suddenly, another chameleon approaches, ready for a fight. The upper cell layer in the creature's skin becomes excited and turns bright.

Milan Zygmunt/Shutterstock

TAKE NOTES

Usually, it's an adult male that changes hues, with the exact coloration depending on the length of the light's waves. When relaxed, teeny crystal-like structures inside the creature's skin cells are close together, and the structures reflect cool colors with short wavelengths like blue. When excited, the structures spread out. Then hot colors like red get reflected. Unlike animals that change color to hide, the chameleon changes to communicate mood. Its brightness attracts mates, too.

PASSAGE 2 EXPOSITORY TEXT

Changing Their Look

Have you ever been startled by an animal's sudden movement, such as a bird in a tree? An animal often blends into a natural background, difficult to detect, based on its coloration. Chemicals called pigments may produce this camouflage, or the color may come from structures in the animal's cells that reflect light waves.

One sea creature that blends in with its environment is a nudibranch. This small sea creature lives near coral. It hides by becoming the same colors of the coral. The nudibranch first eats the coral, ingests its pigments, and stores the pigments in its skin and intestines, so the color of the coral shows through.

CONNECT TO CONTENT

_____

_____

_____

_____

_____

_____

_____

_____

_____

_____

_____

_____

_____

_____

_____

_____

_____

Another sea creature that blends in with its environment is a seahorse. This ocean animal is not a strong swimmer, so it hides from predators by taking the color of the undersea area it inhabits.

A third creature that also blends in with its environment is a walking stick, or stick bug. However, a walking stick does not only use color camouflage. It takes the shape of its surroundings, too. This insect easily hides in plants, especially given its plantlike coloration.

In nature, anything increasing chances of survival is called an advantage. Living things develop advantages because those without advantages tend to die off. This is a process called natural selection. Animals without advantages often don't live long enough to have offspring.

(t) Dray van Beeck/Shutterstock; (b) KeithSzafranski/Getty Images

COMPARE THE PASSAGES

Review your notes from "Colorful Chameleons" and "Changing Their Look."
Record how the information in both passages is alike.

Colorful Chameleons	Changing Their Look

Synthesize Information

Think about what you learned in both texts. How does this information
help you understand why some animals must adapt to changes in their
environment? Write your ideas in your reader's notebook.

CHECK IN 1 2 3 4

RESEARCH MIMICRY

Camouflage is the ability to blend into surroundings. It is a type of adaptation. Another form of adaptation that helps animals survive is mimicry, the ability to copy other animals' traits. Some moths, for example, have developed patterns on their wings that look like giant eyes. The "eyes" confuse predators. Some animals have survived by becoming brightly colored like venomous snakes other animals have learned to avoid.

Cuckoo birds lay eggs that mimic the color and size of the eggs of other birds. Cuckoos then hide their eggs in the nests of other birds. Cuckoos also have developed belly feathers that mimic those of raptors. Raptors are birds of prey that eat smaller birds.

With a partner, research how mimicry helps cuckoos survive. Consider these clarifying questions: *Why might cuckoos lay eggs in the nests of other birds? Why might cuckoos have bellies like raptors?*

As you conduct research, take notes in your reader's notebook. Use reliable print and digital sources. Remember to cite your sources.

Discuss your findings as a class.

One cuckoo bird egg next to three marsh warbler eggs in the same nest, Russia.

Reflect on Your Learning

Talk About It Reflect on what you learned in this unit. Then talk with a partner about how you did.

I am really proud of how I can _____

_____

_____

_____

Something I need to work more on is _____

_____

_____

_____

_____

My Goal Set a goal for Unit 5. In your reader's notebook, write about what you can do to get there.

Share a goal you have with a partner.

Argumentative Writing Rubric

Score	Purpose, Focus, and Organization (4-point Rubric)	Evidence and Elaboration (4-point Rubric)	Conventions of Standard English (2-point Rubric begins at score point 2)
4	• stays focused on the purpose, audience, and task • makes a claim that clearly supports a perspective • uses transitional strategies, such as words and phrases, to connect ideas • presents ideas in a logical progression, or order • begins with a strong introduction and ends with a strong conclusion	• effectively supports the claim with logical reasons • has strong examples of relevant evidence, or supporting details, from multiple sources • uses elaborative techniques, such as examples, definitions, and quotations from sources • expresses interesting ideas clearly using precise language • uses appropriate academic and domain-specific language • uses different sentence structures	

Score	Purpose, Focus, and Organization (4-point Rubric)	Evidence and Elaboration (4-point Rubric)	Conventions of Standard English (2-point Rubric begins at score point 2)
3	• generally stays focused on the purpose, audience, and task • makes a claim that mostly supports a perspective • uses some transitional strategies, such as words and phrases, to connect ideas • presents ideas in a mostly logical progression, or order • begins with an acceptable introduction and ends with a sufficient conclusion	• mostly supports the claim with some logical reasons • has some examples of mostly relevant evidence, or supporting details, from multiple sources • uses some elaborative techniques, such as examples, definitions, and quotations from sources • generally expresses interesting ideas using both precise and general language • mostly uses appropriate academic and domain-specific language • mostly uses different sentence structures	

Argumentative Writing Rubric

Score	Purpose, Focus, and Organization (4-point Rubric)	Evidence and Elaboration (4-point Rubric)	Conventions of Standard English (2-point Rubric)
2	• stays somewhat focused on the purpose, audience, and task, but may include unimportant details • does not make a clear claim or does not completely support a perspective • uses few transitional strategies to connect ideas • may present ideas that do not follow a logical progression, or order • may begin with an inadequate introduction or end with an unsatisfactory conclusion	• shows some support of the claim with logical reasons • has weak and inappropriate examples of evidence or does not include enough sources • may not use elaborative techniques effectively • expresses some interesting ideas, but ideas are simple and vague • uses limited academic and domain-specific language • may use only simple sentence structures	• has a sufficient command of grammar and usage • has a sufficient command of capitalization, punctuation, spelling, and sentence formation • has slight errors in grammar and usage that do not affect meaning

(bkgd) Valentain Jevee/Shutterstock

Score	Purpose, Focus, and Organization (4-point Rubric)	Evidence and Elaboration (4-point Rubric)	Conventions of Standard English (2-point Rubric)
1	• is not aware of the purpose, audience, and task • does not make a claim or does not support a perspective • uses few or no transitional strategies to connect ideas • does not present ideas in a logical progression, or order • does not include an introduction nor a conclusion	• supports the claim with few logical reasons or does not support the claim at all • has few or no examples of evidence or does not include enough sources • does not use elaborative techniques • has confusing or unclear ideas or does not express any interesting ideas • does not demonstrate a grasp of academic and domain-specific language • consists only of simple sentence structures	• has an incomplete command of grammar and usage • has an incomplete command of capitalization, punctuation, spelling, and sentence formation • has some errors in grammar and usage that may affect meaning
0			• does not have a command of grammar and usage • does not have a command of capitalization, punctuation, spelling, and sentence formation • has too many serious errors in grammar and usage that frequently disrupt meaning

Expository Writing Rubric

Score	Purpose, Focus, and Organization (4-point Rubric)	Evidence and Elaboration (4-point Rubric)	Conventions of Standard English (2-point Rubric begins at score point 2)
4	• stays focused on the purpose, audience, and task • clearly presents and fully develops the central idea about a topic • uses transitional strategies, such as words and phrases, to connect ideas • uses a logical text structure to organize information • begins with a strong introduction and ends with a strong conclusion	• effectively supports the central idea with convincing facts and details • has strong examples of relevant evidence, or supporting details, from multiple sources • uses elaborative techniques, such as facts, examples, definitions, and quotations from sources • expresses interesting ideas clearly using precise language • uses appropriate academic and domain-specific language • uses different sentence structures	

Score	Purpose, Focus, and Organization (4-point Rubric)	Evidence and Elaboration (4-point Rubric)	Conventions of Standard English (2-point Rubric begins at score point 2)
3	• generally stays focused on the purpose, audience, and task • presents and develops the central idea about a topic in a mostly clear and complete way, although there may be some unimportant details • uses some transitional strategies, such as words and phrases, to connect ideas • uses a mostly logical text structure to organize information • begins with an acceptable introduction and ends with a sufficient conclusion	• mostly supports the central idea with some convincing facts and details • has some examples of mostly relevant evidence, or supporting details, from multiple sources • uses some elaborative techniques, such as facts, examples, definitions, and quotations from sources • generally expresses interesting ideas using both precise and general language • mostly uses appropriate academic and domain-specific language • mostly uses different sentence structures	

Expository Writing Rubric

Score	Purpose, Focus, and Organization (4-point Rubric)	Evidence and Elaboration (4-point Rubric)	Conventions of Standard English (2-point Rubric)
2	• stays somewhat focused on the purpose, audience, and task, but may include unimportant details • does not clearly present or develop a central idea • uses few transitional strategies to connect ideas • may not follow a logical text structure to organize information • may begin with an inadequate introduction or end with an unsatisfactory conclusion	• shows some support of the central idea with few convincing facts and details • has weak and inappropriate examples of evidence or does not include enough sources • may not use elaborative techniques effectively • expresses some interesting ideas, but ideas are simple and vague • uses limited academic and domain-specific language • may use only simple sentence structures	• has a sufficient command of grammar and usage • has a sufficient command of capitalization, punctuation, spelling, and sentence formation • has slight errors in grammar and usage that do not affect meaning

Score	Purpose, Focus, and Organization (4-point Rubric)	Evidence and Elaboration (4-point Rubric)	Conventions of Standard English (2-point Rubric)
1	• is not aware of the purpose, audience, and task • does not have a central idea • uses few or no transitional strategies to connect ideas • does not follow a logical text structure to organize information • does not include an introduction nor a conclusion	• supports the central idea with few facts and details or does not support the central idea at all • has few or no examples of evidence or does not include enough sources • does not use elaborative techniques • has confusing or unclear ideas or does not express any interesting ideas • does not demonstrate a grasp of academic and domain-specific language • consists only of simple sentence structures	• has an incomplete command of grammar and usage • has an incomplete command of capitalization, punctuation, spelling, and sentence formation • has some errors in grammar and usage that may affect meaning
0			• does not have a command of grammar and usage • does not have a command of capitalization, punctuation, spelling, and sentence formation • has too many serious errors in grammar and usage that frequently disrupt meaning